5.29

2956

92   Stambler, Irwin
WAL
         Bill Walton, super
         center

DATE			
MAR 10 '77	MAY 20 '80		
MAY 10 '78	APR. 2 7 1982		
NOV 30 '78	OCT 14 '85		
FEB 4 '80	FEB 2 '88		
FEB 28 '80	FEB 16 '88		
MAR 31 '80	JAN 2 9 '92		
APR 17 '80	FEB 5 '92		
MAY 23 '80	FEB 24		
MAY 23 '80			
DEC 17 '80			
APR 3 '81			
MAY 8 '81			

Bill Walton: Super Center

About the Book

Few men have looked better on a basketball court than tall Bill Walton. As author Irwin Stambler describes him in this memorable sport biography: "At one point he went high above the basket to pick up a rebound and, still off the floor, fired a clothesline straight outlet pass ahead to a streaking Keith Wilkes, whose lay-up made the lead 10–2. . . . Leaping high in the air like a ballet dancer, his shoes five feet off the hardwood floor, he threw out his left hand to meet the spinning ball just as it arched off the board and somehow slapped it back down through the net. . . ." But off the court Walton sometimes puzzles or angers his fans. In this book Stambler also discusses a Walton whose life-style is different from the traditional image of the superstar athlete.

BILL WALTON

SUPER CENTER

by Irwin Stambler

G. P. PUTNAM'S SONS, NEW YORK

Library of Congress Cataloging in Publication Data
Stambler, Irwin. Bill Walton, Super Center.
(Putnam Sports Shelf) Includes index.
1. Walton, Bill, 1952-   —Juvenile literature.
2. Basketball—Juvenile literature. [1. Walton, Bill,
1952-   2. Basketball—Biography] I. Title.
GV884.W3S82   1976   796.32′3′0924   [B]   [92]   75-35931
ISBN 0-399-20490-3   ISBN 0-399-60980-6   lib. bdg.

Contents

1 Tower of Strength

The adrenaline was flowing. The capacity crowd in the Los Angeles Sports Arena that March night in 1974 vibrated with applause, yells, school cheers awaiting the start of another showdown between longtime crosstown rivals USC and UCLA. The game would decide the championship of the Pacific 8 Conference.

Both the University of Southern California and the University of California at Los Angeles had identical 11–2 records, and the season's play had indicated this might be USC's first chance in a decade to crumple the fabulous UCLA Bruin dynasty and go on to vie for the national title in the NCAA postseason tournament. Both teams were in the top ten in the national rankings, but UCLA, for one of the rare times in recent history, was not number one. USC was finishing a great season, one in which it had topped conference statistics in several categories. Still, UCLA had Bill Walton.

The bands played, the cheerleaders danced and pinwheeled, and the shouts crescendoed as the referee stood at center court, holding the tan sphere between the two towering figures: Walton and his less-heralded counterpart, Mike Westra of the Trojans. Flipping the ball upward, the referee stepped back as the redheaded UCLA center soared high above, easily outreaching the stretching fingertips of Westra to tap the ball to a blue-clad teammate. Walton's margin over his opponent amazed some experts, for he measured only an inch taller than the six-foot-ten inch USC player.

Seconds later USC fans yelled with delight as agile guard Gus Williams stole the ball from UCLA and flashed quickly in for the first score. Perhaps it was an omen. In the past USC had been one of the few teams able to upset some of John Wooden's championship teams of previous years. Could this be the start of their first-ever win over a Walton-led team?

The answer came quickly. UCLA swept downcourt to tie the game and then grouped behind Walton for an almost unbelievable show of combined offense and defense. One moment Walton was in the low post at the USC end, hitting lay-ups or hook shots or passing off to cutters; the next he was at the other end, blocking the middle with his impressive form and shouting directions to his co-defenders to counter the Trojan offense. At one point he went high above the basket to pick up a rebound and, still off the floor, fired a clothesline straight outlet pass ahead to a streaking Keith Wilkes, whose lay-up made the lead 10–2.

A short time later Walton screened out Westra on

a USC shot and drew a foul from the desperately lunging center. Moments after that he stole the ball from USC near the Trojan basket and, looking one way, flipped the ball the other to forward Dave Meyers, who scored a "back-door" lay-up. Once more USC got only one shot, and UCLA worked the ball to the ever-moving Walton for another basket. At the five-minute mark UCLA had 14 points, and USC, one of the best shooting teams in the country, had its lonely two points.

USC coach Boyd tried everything—shuffling his players, taking time-outs to regroup, changing strategy —but everywhere Trojan players went Walton seemed to get there first.

On the attack Bruin guards and forwards let fly with lob passes from all parts of the court: 20 feet, 30 feet, even 40 feet. Trojan players sometimes turned to watch the flight of the ball far beyond their reach. And as it dipped toward the basket, momentarily seeming to be heading out of bounds, suddenly Walton was there. With split-second timing he sprang straight up, his hands sometimes extending out almost in line with the top of the backboard. For seconds he seemed suspended in midair as he scooped in the sphere and in one flowing motion dropped it down into the net.

To Trojan fans it didn't seem possible he could go up dizzyingly high again and again as the game progressed to match perfectly his leap with a projectile thrown from half the court away. But he did, and each time friend and foe gasped at how easy he made it seem. No one else could do it, not any of the six-five

9

to six-nine Bruins and Trojans. Not even Westra with his imposing height could handle a long lob pass successfully more than a few times a game.

Nor was Walton's defensive work less frustrating for the Trojans. In a typical play, six-nine Clint Chapman, a superb USC forward, got set for a shot, then saw the tall redhead looming abruptly before him. Big Bill was grimacing and waving his long hands in front of Chapman's eyes. Startled, Clint hurried the shot so it barely hit the rim. Grabbing the rebound, Walton again started the UCLA fast break, trailing the play as Keith Wilkes 15 to 20 feet ahead went up for one of his patented lay-ups. It was one of these rare occasions when the All-American forward's timing slipped; the ball spun into the webbing, then out. But swiftly Walton was there, catching the crowd and USC off guard, somehow having covered a quarter of the court in a fraction of a second.

Leaping high in the air like a ballet dancer, his shoes five feet off the hardwood floor, he threw out his left hand to meet the spinning ball just as it arced off the board and somehow slapped it back down through the net. The crowd gasped as Walton's hurtling form flew past the baseline and out almost to the first row of seats, hitting the concrete floor with a thud. Grinning, Walton bounced up almost immediately, rushing full speed to the other end to harry the Trojan attack.

Rattled, USC missed another single try and hardly had the chance to take a breath when Walton was taking a pass near their basket and outmuscling Westra to hook in another score. USC somehow managed to get past the Bruin zone press and man-to-man guarding to get a few baskets, but guard Andre McCarter soon dribbled into forecourt, passed a high arching lob which Walton took some eight to ten feet in the air and guided in for his sixth basket in six tries.

And still the agony continued for USC. Westra shot from outside, having given up trying to match Walton under the boards, and the big redhead cleared the rebound, starting a play that led to his putting another field goal in at the other end. USC's Dan Anderson, usually a sensational outside shooter, put one up only to see Walton arch high in the air to bat the ball harmlessly away far short of the basket. With 7:13 to go in the half, everyone knew it was all over. Walton alone had outscored USC 14–8, and had a hand in most of the other thirteen points made by his teammates in that time. The TV announcer, voice rasping from the rapid pace, reflected, "You get the feeling whenever USC gets a rebound it's something special. USC is the best shooting team in the conference and only gets eight points in thirteen minutes."

At the half the score was 47–13 in UCLA's favor, and after coasting to a final score of 82–52, the Bruins were ready to take part in the prestigious NCAA tournament for the eighth year in succession and the third in a row with Walton at center.

For Walton the game capped a memorable week. It ranked as one of his best efforts and he had realier been named to the United Press International All-American team (along with forward "smooth as silk" Keith Wilkes) for the third straight year, a feat accomplished by only seven players in the twenty-six-year history of the UPI survey. He won almost unanimous endorsement from the 241 sportswriters and sportscasters taking part, receiving 478 out a possible 482 points. This made him the only player in history to be top vote getter three times running.

Commenting on the game, USC mentor Bob Boyd, smiling grimly, called it "the most perfectly played half of basketball by one team I've ever seen."

A visiting coach from another region was awed by Walton. "When Walton wants to play, he can do it all. He can go left; he can go right; he can hook; he can run and pass like a guard; he can take an outside fifteen-footer like a forward. And he's a tower of strength on defense: He can rebound and block and intimidate. If he keeps developing in the pros, he can be even greater than Bill Russell."

There's no doubt the praise and adulation were well merited, but it was not always welcomed by the complicated individual that is Ball Walton. Again and again he has taken pains to point out his belief there is much more to life than athletics. He has stressed he plays basketball because he enjoys it, but he also suggests sports should be kept in perspective.

After an outstanding game in the NCAA finals against Memphis State in 1973, Walton wanted only to be left alone. He told a reporter, "My life as Number thirty-two for UCLA has ended for this season. I'm now Bill Walton, just me, not Bill Walton, basketball player. I don't want to talk about basketball."

His close friend Greg Lee, outstanding guard and,

along with stellar backcourt ace Tommy Curtis and Keith Wilkes, charter members of the "Walton Gang," commented, "Bill kind of resents the attention he gets. He feels it isn't right for people to come after him just because he has exceptional physical abilities."

Curtis agreed. "He doesn't like to talk much about his game. He lets his body do his talking."

Part of Walton's attitude reflected his frustration at being singled out in what he felt should be a team activity. In high school and in college his playing brought smiles to his coaches not just because of his dominating characteristics but because of his unselfishness, his strong desire to be a part of a total team effort. Hogging the ball was not his style. If he saw a teammate in position for a shot or lay-up, he preferred to pass off even though he himself had an equally good opportunity to score. His feelings were expressed to an interviewer in this way: "I think the media perceived me a certain way, attributed to me an importance which was distorted. I mean, UCLA could play without me, but I couldn't play without the other guys. . . ."

Early in his career he told Bill Reed of *Sports Illustrated,* "It hurts me when people talk as if I'm the only player on the team. I wish sportswriters wouldn't ask me anything personally at all. I would like to see them get the whole team together. I don't like to be singled out as an individual because we don't play as individuals, we play as a team."

Still, there's no doubt that Bill Walton is a strong-willed person. He does not accept things because someone in authority says they are so, preferring to turn

13

tters over in his mind and come to his own conclusions. As coach Wooden told the Los Angeles *Times,* "Sometimes with Bill I feel like I'm handling a piece of glass. At times he is an enigma . . . inconsistent, changeable, impatient. But his true nature, the one few people see, is extroverted, open and sincere. He definitely ranks up there in the unusual category. Even though we differed, I like him. I like him a lot."

Marques Johnson, who became an important cog in the 1974 UCLA team even though only a freshman forward, seconded the coach. Bill's "not at all like I thought he'd be, you know, with his basketball reputation and the things he's said. I guess I expected him to be aloof, above the rest of us. No way. He's real friendly. I dig him . . . and the other guys do, too."

Ironically, it might be said that Walton's feeling that the public should consider him just another team member related to his own intense individuality. He has always had many interests besides sports but has found it difficult to pursue them in privacy. Highly intelligent, he enjoyed his studies and liked classroom work. But it's hard to submerge yourself in a high school or university when your name is on everyone's tongue and your skyscraping, almost seven-foot build makes you highly visible whether walking in a crwd or sitting in a lecture room.

Bill's interest in learning was one reason he shunned multimillion-dollar offers to turn pro after his spectacular junior year at UCLA, when he led the team to a second straight undefeated season and national championship. He consistently maintained a better than B average. He avoided easy courses that might have taken some pressure off combining the needs for studying with the rugged training schedule imposed by the UCLA coaching staff. He demonstrated his interest in education by taking summer courses at Sonoma State College in northern California during 1973. Characteristically, in keeping with his enjoyment of simple ways of living and outdoor life, he traveled the 500 miles from southern California to Sonoma on his bicycle, taking along a sleeping bag so he could camp out under the stars at night.

The favored financial adviser of UCLA players in the early 1970s, Sam Gilbert, agreed with Bill's ideas about earning his BA before considering a pro contract. "He's not ready for it," he said in 1973. "Usually I would not ever help a player turn pro before his senior year. But in Bill's case, things would be different. If he wanted to sign, I would help him, and I'm sure John Wooden would agree with the decision. But Bill Walton is enjoying going to college and everything associated with being a college student."

The value Bill placed on education was indicated again by his actions when he was selected to the Academic All-America athletic team. He appeared in the unaccustomed dress of jacket, tie, and shoes to accept the award. Conversely, he came in his more normal attire of blue work shirt, blue jeans, and sandals without socks to accept the America Athletic Union's 1973 Sullivan Award for amateur athlete of the year. He thanked AAU president David Rivenes and said a few words to reporters, "This is a great honor. But I'm not receiving it for myself. I happen to be six-eleven and have red hair so I'm the one [from the UCLA team] that's picked out." Then he put on his backpack and rode away from the meeting on his ten-speed bicycle.

Walton's main preoccupation remains developing his own life-style. He puzzled about how athletics fitted into this framework throughout college, and it continued to be a troubling consideration after graduation. Sam Gilbert pointed out in 1973: "He loves the beach and he loves the mountains. Listen, at my house [in Lake Arrowhead] I have four bedrooms, a boat and seven bathrooms. When Bill comes to the house do you think he sleeps there? No, he likes to sleep in the woods. He loves the woods. . . . He's going into the Sierras with his father on a camping trip. He's going to sleep in the snow. He loves nature. . . ." Walton said, "I like to learn from school," but "I don't like being cooped up."

More a student athlete than an athlete who happens to be representing a college, Walton often confused reporters with his discussion of possible careers. Why should he worry about that, they thought, when he's virtually assured of becoming a mutimillionaire once he graduates and signs with a professional team? But Walton in temperament was much closer to his university classmates than to ballplayers. He had a desire to do "good works" and shied away from getting money for money's sake. He often told friends or the few reporters he was willing to talk to that he had doubts about turning pro.

Rather than do that, he told a Los Angeles *Times*

16

reporter in 1974, "I'd rather become a criminal lawyer and offer free service to those in the ghettos who are discriminated against by our society. I could make more of a contribution to mankind that way than by basketball or giving away the money I make. I want to do more with my life than win games."

He also considered other things he might do. "Maybe work on a teaching credential. I'd love to teach. Or maybe put out forest fires. That would be worthwhile."

These conflicting feelings undoubtedly contributed to the misunderstandings and headline-making troubles that befell Bill when he entered the National Basketball Association. But they are not unusual for college students. Recent history shows many promising graduates who shun affluence in favor of idealistic pursuits, though few of those had to shun the lure of instant wealth. Walton, of course, could understand that the $2,000,000 contract arranged by Sam Gilbert with the Portland Trail Blazers would give him the chance to help many less fortunate people in later years. But he probably still had guilt feelings about "selling out," about having to follow orders whether he liked them or not just for pay.

It may also explain the tremendous exuberance he obviously displayed throughout his UCLA years. Though Bill might not like the comparison, he constantly exhibited what was once called the old college spirit. In game after game with the almost all-winning Bruins Walton put his soul into playing. Often when a speedy guard like Curtis, Lee, or McCarter would fast break into the backcourt, Bill would match him stride for stride, yelling encouragement as he headed into position to control the backboard or take a lead pass. Even on the bench he took part, laughing and cheering the others on, sometimes noting to one of the coaches fine points that needed correcting or enemy weaknesses.

Nor did anyone think of him as overly sensitive and moody during those years. He was credited by other Uclans as helping always to relieve the tension with jokes or wisecracks. In the locker room he sometimes sent his cohorts into hysterics by mimicking a blackboard chalk talk but with impossible plays. One such was a "triple pick play" where Walton was set up to take "an easy set shot from thirty feet."

The word also used for him by coach Wooden was "very coachable." Though Walton and Wooden were very dissimilar, they respected each other. Wooden and his assistant coach Denny Crum indicated Bill almost always was willing to accept suggestions to improve his play, though acknowledging that Bill, like other graduating members of the 1973–74 team, suffered the usual cases of "senioritis." In his three years on the varsity Walton rarely got upset at other teams or referees, generally laughing at his own mistakes and even taking very adverse referee's calls in stride.

It was hard to doubt his courage either. For almost his entire college career Walton played in pain, his famous knees subject to the rigors of tendinitis. In order for him to play, he had to follow a strict training routine before and after every game. For a half hour

18

before each game the trainer put heat packs on the knees to loosen up the muscles and ligaments so that the dull, sullen throb would disappear for an hour or so of vigorous motion. Then, as soon as the game was in hand and Bill could go to the sidelines for good, he had to move directly to the locker room for the second part of the treatment—up to a half hour's application of ice packs.

Some experts suggested the knee problem might make Walton too much of a risk for pro ball or might keep him from challenging Jabbar, Cowens, or the other established NBA centers. To this others replied that Bill's doctors said the tendinitis was part of growing up and would eventually subside. In any event, someone like Dave DeBusschere had been a pro all-star for years with a similar problem.

Perhaps more to the point was the question of attitude. Even as Bill made his first appearances on pro courts, experts and sportswriters wondered aloud whether he could generate the same enthusiasm in the more practical count of pro ball. If not, he might fall short of his tremendous potential. But no one could ever take away his unparalleled achievements as one of the greatest college players of all time.

2 Prologue

William Theodore Walton didn't grow up in a ghetto. He didn't lack for food or the necessities of life. He had the advantage of loving parents and a warm, close-knit family. There are parallels to the TV Waltons, except that the real-life Waltons, while far from wealthy, were markedly above the poverty level and grew much taller.

Both of Bill's parents, Ted and Gloria Walton, are above average height. Gloria is tall for a woman, but not excessively so. Ted is a rugged, broad-shouldered individual who towers over most people at six feet four inches. The combination proved a basketball coach's dream. Except for daughter Cathy, who reached only a "measly" five feet eleven inches, all their children easily exceeded six feet. Bruce, the oldest over Bill by a year, shot up to six feet six inches. Bill was already as tall as his father when a high school sophomore; the third son, Andy, three years Bill's junior, eventually topped out at six five. All the children proved fine athletes and basketball players, including Cathy, who starred as center on a women's team at the University of California at Berkeley.

The Bill Walton saga began on November 5, 1952, in San Diego County, a sun-drenched area 125 miles south of Los Angeles and just above the Mexican border. Ted Walton earned a modest living as a social worker. By the time his son was the most sought-after high school basketball player in the nation, he had risen to district chief of the San Diego Department of Public Welfare, supervising the activity of 200 employees and more than 15,000 welfare cases. His salary rose substantially but still was far below what a job with similar responsibility would have paid in private industry. But he had strong sympathy for the underdog and felt he was fortunate to be able to help, a feeling that probably explains his son's strong statements on helping the underprivileged.

Like most Southern Californians, Ted settled his family in the suburbs and drove to and from work. The Waltons' choice was La Mesa, a pleasant middle-class community of one-family homes augmented by the usual shopping centers. The well-kept green lawns and growing trees contrasted with the desertlike scrub growth of the backcountry where Ted and Gloria liked to take their children for picnics and hikes when they were old enough.

There were plenty of friends who wandered in and out of the Waltons' white hillside home as the years went by. Bill and his sister and brothers played the usual round of childhood games and progressed naturally to organized sports when they entered Blessed Sacrament parochial school in San Diego. A local fireman named Frank Graziano, who coached for the fun

21

of it, supervised the school's athletic prgram and watched the development of a succession of Walton boys. Young Bill, already looking somewhat awkward and gangling, eagerly participated in all major sports: baseball, football, and basketball. He was a shy boy, somewhat surprising for someone from a home where both parents were outgoing and had a good relationship with their children. He was generally quiet and stammered on occasion when he talked. Despite the fact that he tried to compensate for his height by walking stoop-shouldered, he forgot that once he was immersed in a game, standing straight and demonstrating good coordination.

By the time he was in the eighth grade at Blessed Sacrament Bill was a starter on several teams. He was an excellent football end, could get behind the secondary better than most, and could take passes above the heads of an opponent's cornerbacks or safetymen. But he really shone in basketball. Though far from short, Bill had not yet attained an extraordinary height, so he was not automatically typed as a center. He demonstrated excellent passing ability and could dribble as well as anyone on the team, so Graziano used him as a combination center and guard. On offense he took the ball downcourt and set up the plays; on defense he was stationed near the basket in the center position to fight for rebounds.

Ted and Gloria were proud of their children's athletic efforts but didn't consider them the sole objective of family life. Education always had high priority, and all of the children were urged to have good study habits. There were always books around the house, and reading was a regular pursuit, as might be expected from Gloria's work as a librarian.

There was much emphasis on doing things as a family. There were family outings, games, and, above all, interest in music. Ted liked to play the piano, and often in the evening when the children were little, he would have everyone gather around after supper for a sing-along. As soon as Bruce, Bill, and the rest were old enough to take lessons, they had instruments in their hands. For a while Ted was surrounded by his own band, with Bill playing baritone horn, Bruce working the slide on a trombone, Andy playing saxophone, and Cathy doubling on drums and flute (or tuba). Ted wouldn't have minded if one of them had taken up music as a career, although he mainly considered it an attribute that would make them more well-rounded individuals.

Still, he enjoyed music more than sports. He told Bill Reed of *Sports Illustrated,* "I never tried to steer my kids into sports. I encouraged them to play, but only as a broadening experience. So wouldn't you know that they all gave up music and wound up in sports."

Bruce entered nearby Helix High in La Mesa in 1965, and the coaches of the varsity football and basketball teams excitedly watched his prowess on the freshman squads. By the time Bill followed the next year Bruce was already being touted as a coming high school all-star in one sport or the other. Bill didn't receive as much attention. He was tall, almost six feet, and getting taller, but he was much scrawnier than the larger-boned Bruce and didn't seem to have as much stamina. He followed his old mentor Frank Graziano's advice by deciding to concentrate only on basketball and did reasonably well on the freshman team.

However, he hurt his left knee, and a medical examination showed he had a torn cartilage. He was operated on and for many weeks had to get around on crutches. Then followed the long period of rehabilitation: the many leg exercises that had to be performed every day, the care to avoid reinjuring the knee, the frustration of a boy at not being able to run or jump or play sandlot games with friends. The knee seemed to be in pretty good shape by the time Bill started his sophomore year at Helix. It still twinged some, and the many months of relative inactivity had taken their toll; it was hard for Bill to keep going for fifteen or twenty minutes straight in practice without feeling weak and winded. Varsity coach Gordon Nash looked him over, then decided the boy needed more seasoning and steady workouts before being ready for varsity. Bill was assigned to the junior varsity team where he spent most of the season. He wasn't downcast about it. He worked hard in practice and spent many of his leisure hours at home polishing up his shooting. He gave steady, sometimes inspired play for the JV. Near the end of the season, coach Nash promoted him to the varsity, where brother Bruce was an established regular.

It was hardly instant stardom for Bill. Nash was interested in him, but at six feet one inch, the boy didn't

24

have any major physical advantages over the team's seasoned players, and he was a novice in varsity competition. Bill spent a lot of time on the bench. He didn't start any games and got into only six contests before the season ended. But his attitude was good; he didn't complain and cheered and urged his team on from the sidelines. Coach Nash watched him closely when he was in and generally approved what he saw. "For a sophomore without any experience, he rebounded pretty well."

Nash was in for a pleasant surprise when he got his team together the next fall to train for the 1968–69 season. There had been a radical change in Bruce's little brother. He had added half a foot to his height. At six foot seven inches, he was two inches taller than Bruce. Nash already knew that Bill had excellent moves and shooting ability. With his increased height he could match up well against any center in the conference. Visions of championships floated in the coach's mind. A tall mobile center is the key building block for any team, and Helix had plenty of good supporting players returning as well.

One question mark was Bill's lack of assurance. He had grown so fast that his weight hadn't kept up. He was six, seven, but at 185 pounds he hardly tipped the scales more than he had at six, one. Even though Nash tried to get his slim charge to pace himself, the running and jumping took a lot out of him. After a while the gaunt redhead would find his legs getting that leaden feeling; it became an effort to get his hands up to ward off an opposing field goal try or to try a shot of his own. Opposing teams tried to help the process along early in the season by stationing large, well-muscled players around Bill to torment him and administer extra physical punishment.

But Bruce was there to help out. At 283 pounds and six foot five inches, he had the build of a football lineman, a role he fulfilled outstandingly both at Helix and in college. Roughhousing adversaries soon found they had Bruce to contend with. The sequence, Bruce told *Sports Illustrated,* began if Bill was taking a going over and "I would look at coach and he would give me a nod." Then, said Gloria Walton, "when the referee wasn't looking, Bruce would give the player an elbow and let him know that the skinny guy was his kid brother."

"After that," said Bruce, "they wouldn't rough up Bill anymore."

Nash worked up a high-low post offense for Helix, with Bill under the basket and Bruce stationed near the top of the key. With every game the operation became more overpowering as Bill picked up confidence and became more polished at shooting. The Walton duo was devastating. If the other team tried to play man for man, Bill could easily twist, jump, or outmaneuver the man guarding him for a score. If they tried to double or triple team Bill, it left the rangy, agile Bruce free for a jumper or a lay-up.

Of course, Nash still had to cope with the need to rest Bill periodically. It took a little while for him to figure out the best way to do this, which may have contributed to Helix's losing two games in the first half of the season. Once he had the pattern established, though, Helix was unstoppable. After losing for the second time in game thirteen, the Walton brothers led Helix to sixteen straight wins. The total included a string of post-season tournament victories that carried Helix to the California Interscholastic Federation title for the entire San Diego region. (CIF is the governing body for most high school athletics in California, the only exceptions being a few city districts, such as Los Angeles and San Francisco, which don't belong to CIF.) Bill, despite spending a fair amount of time on the bench resting in all the games, still led the team in rebounds and scoring. College scouts were already coming to watch as Bill's fame spread far beyond his home area. He was named to the All-CIF first team for San Diego and also was voted to the national all-star prep team.

Some observers wondered if his effectiveness might be reduced the following year when Bruce would no longer be there. However, one factor no one could foresee was Bill's continued physical development. It was, in a way, an embarrassment to the retiring youngster that his already noticeable development did not stabilize. He kept right on growing, tacking on a half inch to an inch every month or two. By the fall of 1969, he measured six ten and a half. His features earned him the nickname of Mount Helix from his classmates, a designation that probably didn't bring a smile to his face.

Equally important, he was putting on weight. None of the Walton children ever lacked an appetite. Like

27

his sister and brothers, Bill always packed a prodigious amount of food into his expanding frame, and Gloria Walton cheerfully obliged with hearty meals. Though an avowed vegetarian by the time he left UCLA, Bill in those years eagerly devoured all kinds of dishes. For breakfast he often ate several hot dogs or hamburgers, and evening meals usually featured generous portions of steak or roast. Bill, who attributed his phenomenal growth to his mother's cooking, returned for his senior year weighing some 215 pounds. The extra pounds weren't evident, what with Bill's added three and a half inches, but it made a difference in his durability. He was definitely stronger, could hold his own against pushing or shoving opponents under the basket, and found he could go at top speed a lot longer without feeling weary or winded. Helped by the coaching staff, he also had learned to conserve energy by not charging up and downcourt as often. After a good outlet pass, for instance, he didn't have to keep pace with the guards or forwards but could trail the play either for a follow-up tip in or a move to the low post while the other team members worked the ball among themselves until he was ready.

Other teams only had to watch Walton and Helix in action the first few games to know their worst fears had materialized. Helix wasn't just as good as the previous year's champions; it was obviously better. Walton was just about unbeatable on the boards—twisting, turning, springing away above the rim to spear the basketball in those long, slender fingers. His passes to teammates were almost always straight and unerring. His shooting average consistently was well above 50 percent, and as the season progressed, it seemed certain he would be the scoring leader not just for the team, but for the league and even the entire country.

Walton could play longer without needing a substitute, but Coach Nash didn't need to worry about that so much. The team dominated its foes so much that in most cases Walton could be pulled out long before the end of the game. Word of the Helix marvels spread to all corners of the land as Walton's exploits were featured in stories in magazines and newsletters read by high school and college coaches and talent scouts.

At Helix and in the city of San Diego Bill was a celebrity. The problems of being in constant public view began to multiply, and he didn't like it. Almost every move he made now seemed to be monitored by unseen eyes. On one occasion he was particularly upset when, after escorting a girl to a concert, he found it mentioned the next day. As Bill told a reporter, he complained to coach Nash, "I can't do anything without reading it in the papers." At Bill's request the coach agreed to talk to reporters asking for interviews and try to keep most of them from bothering him.

But nothing seemed to bother Bill on the court. As the 1969-70 season went by, Walton steadily improved on an already-unparalled series of performances. Opposing coaches tried everything—double teaming him, triple teaming, using zone defenses. Nothing worked. Whenever an opponent got close to the Helix basket, there was Walton bulking before him. It didn't take many minutes into a game before the other team's center, as well as forwards and guards, started looking for Bill even before he came up to challenge them. Just the thought of his possible actions led to breakdowns in timing, missed passes, and off-target shots.

When Bill was on the attack, he was an almost irresistible force. There seemed almost no way the other team's big men could screen him out. His sudden feints at other times would catch a defender moving the wrong way or coming down as Bill was going up for a high percentage shot. Not that Bill put the ball up that often. He liked to see the Helix forwards and guards get their share of chances and set them up again and again with fast-break starting outlet passes or, close in, perfect short or bounce passes. And with all his team play, the statistics still showed Bill as the top point getter. Though he tried fewer baskets than most centers with his awesome advantages would attempt, he rarely missed. On occasion his field goal percentage nudged up toward 80 and 90 percent. Rare was the Helix game Bill finished with fewer than 25 or 30 points. He offset those with other games where his totals went well past 30. Equally impressive, his rebounding easily led the league, and his total rebounds per game often matched his total points scored.

Helix breezed through its regular schedule. Fans and sportswriters alike talked about the team's string of victories. Helix won 10, 20, 30 in a row as the season went by without a loss. Long before the season ended, the question wasn't whether Helix would win its league, but if anyone could keep them from a second straight regional crown. The only chance, it was generally agreed, was if there was an accident to Helix's supercenter. He did have knee problems, of course, and some observers wondered if he could keep taking the punishment, a question that has been raised more than a few times in Walton's career. But nothing did go wrong. Every game Bill was there, active, exuberant, unstoppable.

When the season came to a close and the best teams in the district readied for postseason play, Helix was the overwhelming favorite. As expected, coach Nash's boys won all the preliminary games and made the finals. Their opponent was Chula Vista High School from 20 miles south of San Diego. Though Chula Vista seemed to have little chance on paper, it was still a very good team, one that had beaten many worthy adversaries to make the championship game. Certainly if anyone in the region could stop Helix, Chula Vista seemed to have the best personnel to do it.

There was no lack of excitement in the area. When the two teams arrived for warm-up practice in the sports arena, they were greeted by the cheers of some 6,450 fans. The crowd, one of the largest to watch a high school game in the state, was vibrant with excitement and activity. On opposite sides of the court, cheerleaders urged on student sections in a deafening contest of school yells. If fan support could do it, Chula Vista promised to be a fair match for Helix.

The noise reached fever pitch as Walton squared off against Chula Vista's center for the opening tip-off.

But the eager expression of Chula Vista supporters turned to despair as Bill began to get Helix moving inexorably past its rivals. He seemed to be everywhere on the court, as usual, controlling the boards at both ends, running, passing, shooting, and even stealing the ball from attacking players on occasion. Helix fans happily sang school fight songs, and some raised fingers in unison indicating their team was number one.

But there were people scattered in the audience who didn't look at all like students. Nor were they chanting or applauding activities on the floor. They were scouts for the many colleges and universities who wanted to know more about Helix's star attraction. As they sat there unobstrusively, they got ready to note how Walton reacted under the pressure of a big game, whether he demonstrated unexpected skills or had obvious flaws on offense or defense. For them only Walton mattered; who won the game was immaterial.

The scouts sat on the edges of their seats, many of them awestruck by the power and grace of the lanky teenager. Some could see a few problem areas, but nothing that wouldn't yield to good coaching and proper practice. They watched as the all-too-familiar picture to San Diego high school coaches unfolded, with Walton picking the enemy defense apart by scoring from almost every angle and almost literally smothering the Chula Vista attack at the other end. Again and again he left the floor as if propelled by springs to stop a shot in midair and slap it like a handball to a teammate. When Chula Vista did get the ball safely away, if it didn't go in the basket, it almost always ended up in the beckoning hands of the smiling redhead.

When the game was over and Helix was crowned district champion for a second straight year, Walton's totals told the story. He had scored 26 points, blocked 16 shots, and pulled down a fantastic 33 rebounds. Helix had followed his lead to win its thirty-third straight game against no losses and a two-year unbeaten string of 49. In those 33 games in 1969–70, Walton had shattered almost every school, league, and district record in sight. He scored 958 points for an average of 29 points a game, an all-time San Diego area prep scoring record. His shooting percentage was over 70 percent. In rebounds, he generally was high man for each Helix game and finished the season with a 22.4 average. Naturally, he was a unanimous selection for first team All-CIF in San Diego and, for the second straight year, chosen for the national All-America team.

The scouts who had watched the championship game and those who learned of it from news reports passed the word along: to recruit Walton if at all possible. So the deluge began. Week after week representatives of schools across the United States made their pilgrimage to San Diego. They contacted coach Nash, Bill's teammates, and the Walton family and impressed on everyone the advantages of their particular place of learning. Some of the best-known names in college basketball coaching circles began appearing at the Walton dinner table in La Mesa—including a man named John Wooden.

3 Enter John Wooden

John Wooden became a legend in the space of a decade. From a reasonably successful coach with a good, if not outstanding, record, his successes of the 1960s brought him recognition as one of the greatest basketball mentors of all time. His reputation as a teacher of the fine points of basketball caused dozens of the best young prospects in the nation to seek him out. Wooden himself was a gracious host if prospective players visited the campus, but he rarely went personally to influence them. For ones of extraordinary talent, though, he made exceptions.

Not that UCLA didn't actively recruit new players. Wooden knew a top-flight team had to do some of that if it were to remain in major contention. But he never encouraged excessive pressure or the offering of unusual inducements, feeling that academic excellence of a school coupled with an outstanding sports program provided strong arguing points. In general, he left most of the contact work to his assistants. They, in turn, often received suggestions, scouting tips, and unsolicited help from UCLA's many interested alumni. For instance, one famous alumnus, Dr. Ralph Bunche, then U.S. ambassador to the United Nations, wrote a letter to a young New York prep star in the mid 1960s outlining the advantages of attending UCLA.

The New York player was Lewis Ferdinand Alcindor, Jr., now known as Kareem Abdul-Jabbar. Reports of his phenomenal ability had gone over the college coaching grapevine when he was not yet finished with high school, just as happened later with Bill Walton. Thus when Alcindor's coach at Power Memorial, Jack Donohue, wrote Wooden noting he and his star center, then a junior, were going to attend the Valley Forge Basketball Clinic in Philadelphia, it helped make the UCLA coach decide to accept an invitation to address the meeting. Donohue said he wanted to talk to Wooden about "his big fellow." In the discussion Wooden simpy expressed interest without making any special offers. But he shrewdly suggested that Alcindor, who he knew would be deluged with scholarships and awesome pressures from other schools, visit UCLA first in his senior year. It was a bit of psychology. For one, the last school tends to be freshest in a person's mind. For another, Wooden wanted Alcindor to arrive as late as possible so the new basketball arena being built on campus, Pauley Pavilion, would be nearer completion. He wanted Alcindor to understand his talents would be showcased in one of the newest and most impressive courts available.

Even as Alcindor announced his intention to attend UCLA on March 4, 1965, in a New York press conference, Wooden was guiding his team to a second straight NCAA championship. In 1964, he had won his first ever with a relatively small but scrappy team that featured such great outside shooters and ball handlers as Gail Goodrich and Walt Hazzard. Without a tall center, the team capitalized on excellent defense, including Wooden's 2-2-1 zone press, and blazing quickness that made its fast break a delight to watch to win 30 in a row, capped by a 98–83 humbling of a taller Duke University team in the NCAA final game. Against Duke, as it had done so often in the season, UCLA spotted them an early lead, then came back later with a sudden spurt (16 straight points near the end of the first half) that shattered the other team's morale.

For the first time Wooden had upset the maxims of the basketball establishment. Things never were to be the same again. After the Duke game, Bill Sims of the Kansas City *Star* wrote, ". . . they proved the experts wrong who contend you can't win anymore without a lot of height. All the Bruins had was a group of big men, not in stature but in talent, desire, hustle and the ability to come from behind once again in the most important game they've played." Wooden showed he could win without big men; with Alcindor and, later, Walton, he demonstrated he could take maximum advantage of tall players as well.

Soon after Alcindor's 1965 announcement, capacity crowds in Portland, Oregon, watched UCLA humble Wichita State and Michigan in order for another NCAA crown. Once again it was finesse, the shooting and defending of Goodrich, Keith Erickson, Freddie Goss, and other relatively small men, that won the day. It was the kind of basketball Wooden had always emphasized, a style that employed some techniques he had learned from his coach at Purdue University, Ward "Piggie" Lambert, where he was an All-American guard three years in a row, 1930–31–32.

So well known was Wooden for his fast-paced style that many experts wondered whether he had the flexibility to accommodate his team's strategy to a really big man like Alcindor. Wooden himself noted the extra pressure he felt when Lew selected UCLA. Basketball authorities stated flatly that any team acquiring the seven-footer's services should be a shoo-in for three straight national titles once he reached the varsity. Wooden wrote in his book *They Call Me Coach,* "There was no doubt in my mind of Lewis's potential. If there was doubt of any kind, it was in my ability to live up to the forecasts that were immediately made. . . . I didn't know exactly how I could use a big man to the best advantage. I had never had a chance to experiment."

Wooden had a year to work things out while Alcindor served his apprenticeship on the freshman team. If it had been a half dozen years later, UCLA would have had the giant youngster at center in his novice season, for rules were changed to let freshman play on the varsity by then. (The rule change came a year too late for Walton as well.) It might well have meant a third straight championship in 1965–66. As it was, Wooden had a rebuilding year, having lost Goodrich, Erickson, and the other stars of the previous two years through graduation. But UCLA had far from a bad year. Wooden took his relatively green team, which, as usual, lacked height, to second place in the Pacific 8 conference. Its record was 10–4 in the Conference and 18–8 overall, a result that would have satisfied most teams in the nation. The Alcindor-led freshman team, however, went undefeated.

Wooden watched Alcindor play when he got the chance and sometimes consulted with the freshman coach on training methods to improve Lew's already-awesome game, and he thought and rethought how best to use the center's abilities. He talked to other coaches who had experience with tall centers, watched endless reels of game films of other teams, filled up pages in his notebook with possible plays for his embryo superstar. And he considered how to plan his workouts to prepare for a different style of play from the one his teams were used to without losing sight of his continual stress on learning the fundamentals. It was a self-educational process that had import not only for Alcindor, but for other dominating centers that might come Wooden's way in the future. Big Lew readied Wooden for Big Bill.

By the time Alcindor turned out for his first practice sessions as a varsity player Wooden had figured out his approach. As he wrote in *They Call Us Coach:*

In this, my first chance to build around an outstanding big man, I scrapped my whole offense and went to a totally different one than I had ever

38

used. A complete low post offense placed the center deep, near the basket and well inside the free throw line. I had used a double post, a double low post, a double high post in a limited way, but never a single low post. To take full advantage of his height, I wanted Lewis Alcindor no farther from the offensive basket than he could reach. I almost wanted him to be able to stick his arm out and dunk the ball—no more than eight feet away.

Wooden's ideas, as the sports world well knows, worked brilliantly. The team was even younger and inexperienced than the previous year, but Alcindor's imposing presence more than made up for that. Bolstered by his overpowering scoring ability and catlike rebounding prowess, the supporting cast, which included such people as Lynn Shackelford at forward and Mike Warren and Lucius Allen, quickly picked up poise and confidence. Coming events cast their warning shadow for the basketball world in the first game when UCLA routed its traditional rival USC, 105–90, in a nonleague game.

From then on, UCLA and Alcindor proceeded through the college ranks like a juggernaut. For the second time in Wooden's career, one of his teams completed an entire season, including the NCAA tournament, without a loss. But the 30–0 record of the first Alcindor year was considerably more one-sided than the 1963–64 team's string. With Lew's skyscraping size making ball control under both baskets almost child's play for him, UCLA rarely had to breathe hard.

There were few even relatively close games. UCLA didn't beat teams; they demolished them, storming past four of the nation's top teams in the NCAA tournament with almost predictable ease. In the semifinals at Louisville, the Bruins walloped a good Houston team, which featured a promising young center of its own, Elvin "Big E" Hayes, 73–58. In the finals it was more of the same as UCLA vanquished Dayton, 79–64. With that win, Wooden teams had marked up a string of twelve straight victories in the sudden death competition of NCAA play, already a record even at that early stage of what is known as the Wooden Decade.

The next year was almost a repeat, except for one famous pause. That was the classic confrontation of UCLA and Houston at the Astrodome before the largest crowd ever to watch a basketball game, about 50,000, and a coast-to-coast TV audience. Elvin Hayes had his revenge for the NCAA loss as Houston upset Big Lew and his mates, 71–69. But the win was tainted a little by the fact that Alcindor had to play with an eye that had been painfully injured a little earlier in another game. For the week before the game he had to stay in a dark room with a patch over the eye and couldn't practice with the team.

Other than that, it was another perfect season. UCLA won almost half its regular season games with more than 100 points per game. The big question mark that remained was the expected rematch of Houston and UCLA in postseason play. The moment came in the semifinals, a draw that made the finals an anticlimax, as was to happen when the Walton Gang faced

North Carolina State in 1974. But by then Alcindor was back in top playing condition, and Wooden and his staff once more proved their position as first-rank basketball technicians with a defense that almost paralyzed the Houston offense.

Against Houston, Wooden devised a defense formation known as the diamond and one with four players deployed in a 1–2–1 pattern. The last "one" of the diamond was Alcindor, who stayed back guarding the basket. The roving "one" was assigned to Lynn Shackelford. While the diamond foursome stayed within given sections of the floor, Shackelford had one job, to go wherever Elvin Hayes went. He was told to pick up Hayes as soon as he came up court and stick so close to him it would be almost impossible for the other Houston players to pass him the ball. This harrying tactic could backfire, Wooden knew, if Hayes got a step on the defender or caught him leaning the wrong way and shot past him. But then he would find Alcindor waiting for him. The strategy worked beautifully. The Big E didn't score a basket until slightly past the middle of the first half. His teammates kept Houston close for a while, but the pressure told, and UCLA went on a tear in which it outscored Houston 21–5. By the end of the first half Houston was thoroughly demoralized. UCLA won by more than 30 points, 101–69.

It was a stunning performance in every way. Sports experts across the land enthused over the talent of UCLA and the acumen of John Wooden and quoted Houston coach Guy Lewis: "That was the greatest exhibtion of basketball I've ever seen." The stories couldn't fail to impress high school players throughout the United States who were thinking about their future careers. Certainly the San Diego papers Bill Walton read carried a full share of material on the event. Two days later UCLA whipped North Carolina, 78–55, for championship number four in Wooden's career and still another first: the first time one school won back-to-back NCAA laurels on two different occasions.

The next year, as Bill Walton was just coming into his own at Helix, the sports pages were again filled with the exploits of Big Lew and his all-powerful cast. Wooden had plenty of experienced talent to aid Alcindor–Shackelford, Kenny Heitz, reserve Bill Sweek. But the lure of Westwood for fine players showed in the ranks of newcomers: junior college transfer John Vallely, backup center Steve Patterson, and two agile, big, rugged sophomores, Curtis Rowe and Sidney Wicks. The team was chosen to win again, and it stumbled only once, losing a hard-fought game to USC on the last day of the regular season, 44–46. There were some difficult moments in the tournament, but after a scare from an unheralded Drake team in the semifinals at Louisville, Kentucky, 85–82, UCLA went on to "swallow up" an excellent Purdue squad, 92–72. Alcindor's farewell game was one of his best as he scored 37 points, swept up 20 rebounds, and dominated the boards. While Walton and his Helix crew won its first San Diego title in years, UCLA achieved the first-ever three-straight NCAA victories and John Wooden's fifth national title in six years.

With Alcindor's departure UCLA was expected to come back to the crowd. But Wooden again fooled everyone. He changed the team's offensive style back to the shoot-and-run approach of earlier years, molding it to the abilities of Wicks, Rowe and Patterson. He used a high post offense because the six-nine Patterson had a fine outside touch from the key. And he utilized John Vallely's ball-handling talent for running the attack, giving a new young guard named Henry Bibby leeway for a consistent display of outside shooting from all parts of the floor. The team's 28–2 record wasn't quite as good as the 33–0 season of Walton and Helix High, but the two losses were in conference play, and the team won when it had to. At the end of regular play, UCLA was again Pacific 8 champ and soon national titlist for the fourth year in a row with a win over a taller Jacksonville team, 80–69, in the NCAA finals at College Park, Maryland.

As might be expected, the accomplishments of coach Wooden and his peerless team far overshadowed the efforts of Walton and Helix even in San Diego. At College Park, Maryland, UCLA under Wooden's tutelage was closing out the winningest decade ever for a college team. Athough Bill and his team received some attention in local papers, all the sports section headlines in March went to UCLA's quest for its fourth straight national championship. In nearby Los Angeles and elsewhere in the country UCLA received reams of publicity, but Helix High was never mentioned at all.

But if the pubic had no idea who Bill Walton was, the university and college athletic departments were well aware indeed. The scouts who had followed his career for almost two years verified Bill's skills had become more polished with each game of the 1969–70 season. His name was already being bracketed with Alcindor's—by then, known as Kareem Abdul-Jabbar, an established National Basketball Association superstar. While Wooden was directing the attack on another national title, councils of war at major schools were mapping ways to persuade the San Diego redhead of the glories of their school program. With a prospect like him on campus, UCLA's competitors knew they would finally have a chance to break the growing UCLA stranglehold on college basketball. Many a coach shuddered at the idea of Walton following Alcindor to Westwood.

The inquiries came in thick and fast as Walton's Helix career went into its final, all-winning stage. All the Pac-8 schools, including UCLA, indicated interest. Letters, phone calls, and proposed visits came from campuses both large and small. Bill's father, Ted, who screened them with the help of Helix coach Nash, kept count until he got to more than 110, then gave up. Many recruiters wanted to take the entire Walton family out for dinner at the best restaurants in town. It was a tactic that often worked well with families of players from ghetto areas, and even prospects from relatively affluent homes didn't turn down such an invitation.

But Ted Walton never bowed to pressure. He felt Bill's decision should be made as free from obligation as possible. He also supported his son's desire to stress the educational aspects of any school he considered attending. Ted wanted his children to go to college with the thought of getting a degree, and all of them agreed with him on the importance of doing that. As a result, the choice narrowed down to institutions with good faculties and courses. Not that they had to be in the top ten or twenty academically, but they had to have what Bill and his family considered above-average academic programs. The nice things about it was that Bill could consider schools on that basis. He had a good grade point average at Helix, high enough so he didn't need to be a great athlete to qualify for most universities.

While Ted Walton turned down dinner invitations, he wasn't unwilling to speak to school representatives or have them talk to Bill. But he wanted it done on terms he and his wife had worked out the year before when Bruce Walton was being sought by football coaches from many universities. The main thing, they had decided, was to avoid being obligated to anyone in any way. If officials wanted to discuss Bill's future, fine; but it had to be in such a fashion that no outside money was spent on the Walton family.

So once he, Gloria, and Bill had decided on which schools met Bill's goals, he invited the coach to have dinner at the Walton house. He told reporters, "It's a tradition we began when Bruce was being recruited for football." Any coach given that opportunity was more than happy to accept. Those who made their way to the neat white home on the La Mesa hillside included the top coaches of college basketball. From South Bend, Indiana, came Johnny Dee, director of basketball fortunes of mighty Notre Dame. A hopeful John Boyd spent a pleasant evening trying to convince Bill of the advantages of UCS, dreams of a breakthrough in the frustrating years of being runner-up to Wooden-led team flitting through his mind. But Boyd, a realist, was well aware his crosstown nemesis was also on the Walton guest list.

In due time Wooden appeared at the Walton table. Exactly what the conversation was like that night has never been recorded. Ted Walton has noted that the meal served was one dear to the Waltons' tastes: meat and potatoes. Questions were probably asked about what the training requirements would be if Bill attended Westwood. Wooden may well have told some stories in his soft-spoken manner of some of the interesting moments in the history of his fabulous teams. A discussion of UCLA plays and strategy and how they compared to Bill's experience at Helix may have received a little attention. For the most part, though, it was a social evening, giving Bill a look at the personality of a man who could have a dramatic effect on the future course of his life. At a reasonably early hour Wooden thanked his hosts for their hospitality and made the 125-mile trip back to Los Angeles.

Bill had not given any final reply to any school

when the round of visits was over. In a way, it was a much happier situation than that facing most high school seniors. Most college aspirants had to wait anxiously to see which schools would open their doors to them. In Bill's case it was the other way around. Not only coaches, but also many university officials, worried about is choice. His presence promised a publicity bonanza that could spark added interest among high school college applicants. It also almost guaranteed healthy gate receipts that could support entire sports programs for many institutions.

But Bill also felt a great amount of stress. He had his pick of many of the best schools in the country, and the decision required a tremendous amount of thought. He also had to cope with the irritation of growing attention from radio, TV, and newspaper reporters constantly probing to try to ferret out his choice.

Bill took his time, however. He was kept informed of developments at the various schools, such as what other players might join him on the freshman team. From UCLA he heard that two players whose abilities he was familiar with had enrolled: all-prep guard Greg Lee and a sensational forward from Ventura, Keith Wilkes. Soon after learning of their move, he announced he too would enter UCLA. His reason, he later told reporters: "I felt they offered the best combination of academics and athletics."

4 Learning the Ropes

The Bill Walton UCLA saga began rather quietly in the fall of 1970. Bill registered for classes and bought his schoolbooks without attracting any more attention than usually would be directed at someone rising a foot or more in height above those around him. His presence was duly noted in the UCLA student paper, but he was still an unknown quantity, and the 30,000 other young people thronging the large multi-building campus that nestled in one of the environs of Los Angeles had not yet placed him on any special pedestal.

Besides, it was getting on toward football season. The Walton of interest was brother Bruce who, weighing 265, already had won a starting tackle position on the Bruin eleven. Some local writers suggested that though he was only a sophomore, he might prove a candidate for All-America honors.

Having Bruce on campus naturally made the transition from La Mesa to the student dorms in Westwood somewhat easier for Bill. But Bill had done a good bit

48

of traveling during the summer anyway, so he was used to being away from home. He had agreed to join an Amateur Athletic Union squad that toured Europe playing teams on both sides of the Iron Curtain. He got a look at many new places, but he didn't find them too pleasant.

Most of his AAU teammates were older and more attuned to the restrictions and problems of constant traveling. While almost all had played on college teams, they were launched on careers in the armed forces or in industry by the time Walton met them. Bill was taller than most, but the coach didn't like to take chances on a teenager, and Bill spent most of his time on the bench. In fact, the most memorable part of the trip came when Bill played against his own team. It took place in Czechoslovakia when the local team was shorthanded. Bill was asked to play for them. The Czechs weren't very tall on average, and they didn't have the hard-won polish of the U.S. players, but with Bill on their side things were made more even. For his age Bill put on a fine display of hustling basketball. It wasn't enough to change the outcome. The American team finished on top, but the audience gave Bill an enthusiastic standing ovation.

Soon after Bill was settled at UCLA, he was briefed on what was expected of him by then freshman coach Gary Cunningham. The two got along well. Cunningham, a youthful thirty-one, was a product of UCLA's basketball system. As a starting forward on John Wooden teams of the early 1960s, he made use of a classy outside jump shot to score 919 points, a mark that placed him twelfth on the all-time UCLA scoring list in 1970. He could see that would change soon, however. Rowe and Wicks were back for their senior years, which meant two more candidates for the scoring ranks, and Gary well knew the potential of his latest freshman center.

Cunningham wore two hats, the second being an assistant varsity coach, which established the close liaison needed between Wooden and his future hopefuls. As it happened, Gary moved up with Walton the following year to full-time varsity action when the former number two coach, Denny Crum, moved on to lead the University of Louisville team into play-off contention.

Gary felt it would be a good 1970–71 season. He had the most heralded player since Alcindor on his roster in Walton, and he also knew the other team candidates had high school pedigrees that, except for height, ranked them alongside the slender redhead. As Bill and the others became better acquainted, it seemed obvious they woudn't have many personality problems. Even in practice the others could appreciate Walton's desire to play a team game. The rest of the squad seemed to catch his spirit and avoid the sullen competition for playing time that sometimes marks groups of highly talented athletes.

Bill respected the ability of such players as Greg Lee, Jackson Keith Wilkes, Vince Carson, and Gary Franklin, most of whom were to share in the fortunes of UCLA's varsity for three years. All had been all-league in their respective high schools, and Lee and Wilkes had won national attention.

Lee, at six foot, four inches and 195 pounds, was a good ball handler and outside shooter. At Reseda High in the nearby San Fernando Valley, he averaged 20 points a game as a sophomore, 27.3 as a junior, and 29 as a senior. He was All-West Valley League those three years and was chosen Los Angeles City Player of the Year in his junior and senior years. Wilkes had an unorthodox off-balance outside shot that didn't fit the shooting fundamentals usually stressed by Wooden and his staff. But it had terrorized teams throughout Southern California for all of Keith's high school career, and the UCLA mentors were wise enough not to tamper with success.

Keith had starred as both center and forward in high school, thanks to his great speed and unusual jumping ability for rebounds. At six six, he could concentrate on becoming a great forward and leave the center job to Big Bill. Consistency was his strength, as he had shown first at Ventura High and, in his senior year, at Santa Barbara, averaging 20.7 a game at the first and 24.1 at the second. In 1969 he was selected to the All-Southern-California-CIF first team. He repeated 1970 and was also voted the region's player of the year.

And there were others with credentials almost as impressive: Hank Babcock, All-CIF first team guard from Norte Dame High in Sherman Oaks, California; Dave Cumberland, guard from Santa Maria High who'd played against Wilkes in high school; Ron Werft, captain and forward at North Hollywood High. Less

51

heralded hopefuls also appeared for the tryouts, well-coordinated athletes who might have made the team at another college but had little chance of edging out the superlative talent always attracted to UCLA. As the weeks went by, these fell by the wayside as, indeed, more than half those chosen for that freshman team were to do in the varsity shakedown. But there was never any doubt in anyone's mind about Walton's future.

By late October Gary Cunningham had firmed his squad, and Bill and his teammates settled down to the routine of serious training. Cunningham was in charge and made changes as he saw fit, but his approach naturaly was that used by the varsity. He helped coach Wooden in the drills of the "big team" and was well aware that the precepts laid down by Wooden were the most successful in college basketball history. Bill, Keith, Greg, and the rest were learning the ropes of the Wooden system.

The three things stressed to them constantly were: condition, fundamentals, teamwork.

The importance of conditioning was something Wooden was schooled in during his playing years at Purdue. In more than one key game his coach had told the squad they would win because his training had prepared them to play at top speed the whole game whereas their opponent would start to slow down in the last ten to fifteen minutes. During those years, Wooden later recalled, he often thought, "I may play someone better than I am, but I'll never run against one who is going to be in better condition."

UCLA basketball teams followed this principle to the letter. Walton had been used to exercising and working out in his Helix years, but the schedule at Westwood was far more demanding. There were routines to strengthen the arms and legs and improve breathing, and there was a lot of running. These weren't necessarily much different from what the players were used to in high school, but they were longer and carried each person's body closer to the limits of physical endurance. Much of the body building was worked into the everyday practice drills to make the process of building stamina more interesting.

Many of these drills emphasized the basics: dribbing practice while coaches suggested how changes could be made for more efficient ball handling, foul shooting, outside shooting, passing drills, defensive tactics. There was no emphasis on anything fancy. Again and again the stress was on keeping things simple, but repeating each move so often it became almost automatic. To get the feel of game conditions, almost every practice devoted time to scrimmages. However, there were never full court scrimmages; rather, they were half court situations with varying numbers of players taking part. Sometimes Bill and the others scrimmaged two-on-two, sometimes three-on-three. Even with full five-man teams, the practice was kept to half court because the coaching staff felt this provided more concentrated repetition of the most important facets of the game.

Bill found the practices rugged, but never boring. He and his teammates probably didn't realize how much work went into achieving that. Sometimes the coaching staff would spend hours planning sessions that might last for relatively brief periods. The goal was to break each drill routine into small time periods of ten to fifteen minutes each. Every drill segment was designed to stress fundamentals and movement. Movement was a basic part of the Wooden philosophy. Never stand around in a game, he told his players. Keep things going to make the other team work and, eventually, make a mistake that you can exploit. So the drills always included some running. After Bill would shoot a series of fouls, he had to run a few laps around the gym. Or in passing drills, he and several others would run rapidly upcourt, exchanging short, sharp passes. The passing drills were always designed to move the ball forward in line with Wooden's belief in aggressive playing, in which the ball is worked always forward, never backward.

In many ways the practices were enjoyable. But they were not free from anxiety. As the season neared and the scrimmages took up more of the drills, the pace often made Walton and the others feel they were in the middle of a championship game with the outcome hinging on the way they worked the ball in or shut off the opponent's attack.

Coach Wooden wrote about UCLA's program:

In every facet of basketball, we work on pressure. The opponent provides that during a game. I try to provide it in practice with drills that create game conditions. . . . When a player constantly works under pressure, he will respond automatically to it. For this reason I am confident that what the team does on the weekend in a game relates 100 percent to what it does during the week.

Essentially, I'm more of a practice coach than a game coach. This is because of my conviction that a player who practices well plays well.

One thing the Bruin freshmen didn't have to control with was a play book. The team did use plays which coach Cunningham outlined on a blackboard, but there were not too many of them, and they were relatively simple. The main one worked off a one-guard offense. The point guard, usually Greg Lee, was charged with bringing the ball upcourt. Walton was stationed at the low post near the basket, while the two forwards positioned themselves on the side of the key and the other guard was somewhere between the point guard and the forward line. From this formation guards and forwards tried to set up a shot by cutting toward the basket in various patterns while Walton moved from one side of the basket to the other.

There were other plays the team worked on. One was the lob pass, in which Walton would try to get downcourt fast on offense to leap far in the air for a high arching pass inches from the basket. Another offensive variation was planned after Bill picked off a rebound. His teammates were ready to shift quickly on the attack to receive a Walton outlet pass that would set up the much-favored fast break. On defense, scrimmages stressed both the zone, where each player was assigned a section of floor, taking any opponent that came into it, and the man to man. In general, though, UCLA preferred to use the latter combined with the zone press. Bill's job on defense was to get back to the UCLA basket fast and serve as "last man."

Staying away from fancy plays was a keystone of the Wooden technique. "The main thing I emphasize is fundamentals," he has said, "and I see the fundamentals are taught the way I want."

Every part of the program stressed execution and details. The discipline included insistence on the same grooming standards for all players, the requirement that everyone have the same practice uniforms and eat the same food at the same training table. Close attention was paid to socks and shoes as part of the approach. Right from the start everyone was told of the importance of having the right size footwear and of the proper way to put on socks to avoid blisters.

Year after year UCLA's game plan was predictable. One coach pointed out: "It's hardly worth sending a scout to watch their games. They have a basic set of plays, and they very rarely deviate from them. But they do them so well while you know what's coming you rarely can do much about it."

The UCLA staff had no complaints about young Bill. He always worked hard, and he was willing to listen to advice. Cunningham found him as interested in contributing to good team play as Lew Alcindor had been a few years before. By the time the season was at hand Bill was doing so well in practice, as were

56

some other freshmen, that he would undoubtedly have made the varsity if freshmen had been eligible in 1970.

Cunningham felt he had an almost unbeatable team, although the proof still depended on the pressure of formal competition. The first game was December 4 against El Camino Junior College at Pauley Pavilion preceding the varsity's initial outing against Baylor University. When the frosh game began, few people had bothered to come early, though the house would be filled later that evening. But most of the UCLA staff was on hand to see what the future might hold in store. They weren't disappointed. The Bruins were a little ragged in the early minutes, but once they settled down, with Walton crashing the boards with devastating effect at both ends, El Camino was out of it. The final score was 78–56, one of the lower victory margins for the UCLA Frosh that season. The press paid little attention to that game; the main question naturally was how good the varsity was. The answer was excellent as usual, as Wicks, Rowe, Henry Bibby and Co. demolished Baylor, 108–77.

It was a highly enjoyable season for Big Bill. He was not yet a celebrity and could play basketball to his heart's content without having to cope with reporters' questions or see an unguarded remark make headlines. With each game he became more confident and dominating. He scored in every conceivable way with rebound tap-ins, sweeping hook shots from either side of the basket, and even an occasional outside set shot. To the dismay of opposing guards and forwards he regularly rose up, smiling broadly, to choke off their best attempts. In the team's second game the winning score over hapless Valley State College was 106–60, and from then on it was rare the team didn't go over 100 points a night. Through mid-January, 1971, the team ran up a string of seven straight 100-plus nights with the high being a 77-point edge over Chaffey College as the Bruins won, 128–51.

The team's biggest test was expected to be against the USC freshman team. That school always recruited excellent talent as reflected in the close games it usually fought on the varsity level with John Wooden's super-teams. But USC had no one who could cope with Walton. He led the team in rebounds and played almost perfect defense in the first meeting on February which led to a 78–49 UCLA success. It was an easier win than the varsity's, which just got by a rugged USC squad later that night, 64–60.

When the two freshman teams were rematched in the last game of the season for both on March 13, the results were much the same. Walton received an ovation for his play when he left the court for his usual postgame ice pack treatment on his problem knees. UCLA finished the game with an 86–65 score. As Cunningham had suspected, his team had a year to match that of Lew Alcindor's first year. Walton, Wilkes, and Lee led their aggregation to a perfect 20–0 season, while Alcindor's freshman team had finished at 21–0. Bill's totals weren't quite as impressive as Big Lew's partly because he passed off more often on offense and took fewer shots and party because the team probably ad a little better balance than the earlier

58

one. He scored a total of 362 points and gathered in 320 rebounds, compared to Alcindor's record totals of 696 points and 452 rebounds. The gangling redhead was deadly when he went for the basket, however, connecting on 155 out of 226 field goal tries for a superlative percentage of 62.2 percent.

At season's end there was no question in anyone's mind about the prime mover in the UCLA Frosh success. Bill was awarded the Seymour Armond trophy as the Most Valuable Player.

Meanwhile, the varsity still had some games to play. It had beaten USC for a second time to complete a 14–0 Pacific 8 conference schedule and an invitation to the NCAA tournament. Its regular season record was 25–1, the sole loss coming in an upset by Notre Dame in South Bend in late January, 82–89. The team was not the steamroller it had been in the Alcindor era, and it had several nip-and-tuck battles in the play-offs, most notably a controversial 57–55 squeaker over Jerry Tarkanian's Cal State Long Beach quintet. But when the last whistle sounded in Salt Lake City on March 28, the varsity had vanquished a stubborn Villanova team, 68–62, and John Wooden had achieved a stunning fifth straight national championship and seven titles in eight years. UCLA had become to basketball what the Yankees had once been to baseball. The graduation losses from the 1970–71 team would be severe, but the experts knew that with a player like Walton the dynasty might continue rolling along. It all depended on how the La Mesa youngster responded to the added pressure of varsity competition.

The man with the best viewpoint, coach Wooden, evaluated where Bill stood after the freshman season: "This very maneuverable 6–11 team and defense oriented young man is almost certain to become a real star of the future. He is an exceptional shot blocker and could be the finest outlet man after a rebound to initiate the fast break that I've ever coached. A year of maturity has helped him in regard to the emotional aspects of the game in addition to giving him a little more physical strength.

"His youth and inexperience cause him to play with more emotion than reason at times and this will tend to tire him in tough competition. We are hoping that he will pick up a little more weight as the season progresses which also should help him from an endurance point of view. He should be a team leader in both the press and set defense."

5 Super Soph

When Bill returned to the UCLA campus after the 1971 summer break, he could no longer stay out of the spotlight. UCLA had smashed almost every basketball record in existence and made the school the most watched and envied in the college basketball world. Though Bill steadfastly maintained he was not a one-man team, writers and fans knew he was the fulcrum on which another possible supersquad might be balanced. From the moment he put on his practice suit for his first workouts, he had to fight off legions of reporters who wanted to satisfy the nation's curiosity about the most sensational new player since Lew Alcindor.

As he had with coach Nash at Helix, Bill had asked UCLA's athetic department to keep interview requests to a minimum, and they willingly complied. They naturally wanted to help Bill keep a relaxed outlook on life, and they also knew that a steady flow of newspaper and TV representatives could disrupt not only Wal-

61

ton's concentration on training, but the whole team's.

Walton did talk to a few reporters. He told a *Sports Illustrated* writer: "I realize I can't keep my whole private. My basketball life is open to everyone, but what I do off court for my own recreation and enjoyment is my own business. I do what I want to do, people don't have to know. Even Coach Wooden doesn't know what I do."

He chafed a little under the strict discipline that coach Wooden decreed. "Everybody expects me to be a certain way. They have their idea of what a college ballplayer should be like—short hair and all that—but I'm not like that. I'm myself. I love long hair. I wish Coach Wooden would let us wear it as long as we like to have it. . . . I'm trying to have fun in life and not worry what other people think."

But Bill respected John Wooden, and despite his mild complaints, he appeared for practice with his hair groomed to meet the required standards He might not have agreed with the coach's reasoning, but he could understand it was part of the Wooden system which stressed fundamentals and team rather than individual effort.

Commenting on his short hair edict, Wooden told a reporter, "It's discipline, primarily. A couple of weeks prior to each season I talk to the players and tell them my reasons for wanting their hair short.

"If it's too long, it causes excessive perspiration. That can run down their faces and get in their eyes. You're gonna have to wipe it off. You brush it out of your eyes and get it on your hands. It's harder to hold onto the ball and to keep clean.

"It also takes longer to dry out after a shower. You go out into the night air and you're more susceptible to colds.
It's definitely more difficult to keep a neat appearance, too, and I feel that's important. . . ."

Under the eyes of Wooden and Gary Cunningham, now Wooden's number one assistant, Bill started polishing his skills for a new season. There were some familiar faces from the year before—Keith Wilkes, Greg Lee, Gary Franklin, Vince Carson. But there were a lot of unfamiliar ones. There were a few lettermen back for the '71 national champions, most notably the smooth-shooting ball-handling guard Henry Bibby. The six-one dynamo from Franklinton, North Carolina, had been the spark plug of the surprise NCAA titleholders of '70 and '71. Wooden noted that "Bibby's play in the NCAA finals was overlooked in favor of the more spectacular front-line men [but] it is most unlikely that we would have been the champions without . . . his aggressive defense, outside shooting and endless hustle. . . ."

And, as usual, there were what might be called sleepers, players whom few but the coaching staff had even been aware of before tryouts started. There were athletes who, for one reason or another, had been held out the year before, serving as sort of a varsity taxi squad, or promising performers who had transferred to UCLA from junior colleges. One of these was another giant teenager named Sven Erick Nater, a solidly built dark-haired young man who matched Walton in height at six eleven, and at 238 pounds outweighed him by about 13 to 15 pounds.

Nater's presence was typical of the team's depth and versatility. He was an outstanding athlete, mobile and strong and with a good selection of shots who would have started every game for just about any other team in the nation. The attraction of playing for the number one team in the country and the knowledge that training under Wooden was the finest preparation for professional basketball made many players of ability willing to serve an apprenticeship there. Nater in many ways was a surprising person. He spent his first nine years in Holland, where he was born, and had no high school experience when he entered Cypress California Junior College. But he joined the team and progresed so rapidly in just two years that he was voted to the All-State JC team in his second year. If he had started learning basketball fundamentals as a child, he might well have ranked in Walton's and Alcindor's class. As it was, he was very close to Bill in prowess. Bill often mentioned, when asked about the best center he'd played against, that it had been Nater in practice games.

With Nater and Walton, the 1971–72 team had the tallest brace of centers in the sport. Opposing coaches sometimes shuddered at the thought of what a double post offense using them might do. Generally Wooden preferred to know he had a first-rate center in reserve in case Bill was hurt or got into foul trouble. Once or twice he did play them together for a few minutes more as a surprise for the crowd, it seemed, than to improve what by then usually was an insurmountable UCLA lead.

If Bill was secure in the center spot for the season, some of his mates from the freshman team had stern opposition. Keith Wilkes seemed unbeatable for one forward spot, but he could not ignore two notable juniors, Larry Farmer and Larry Hollyfield, both six five with good credentials from the year before. Farmer, with a relatively slight build, could not outmuscle opponents under the boards, but made up for that with speed, excellent jumping ability, and fine defensive skills. Hollyfield, at 210 pounds, combined quickness with good board strength that could provide Walton with extra rebound help. With that trio, Gary Franklin and Vince Carson, despite impressive freshman achievements, figured to spend most of their time as onlookers.

Bibby had one guard spot sewed up, but the other was a toss-up. Greg Lee had shown great skill at working the ball into Walton through bounce passes, chest-high leading throws, or soaring lobs for some of Bill's breathtaking midair catch-and-score maneuvers. But he had to vie with Thomas Leland "Tommy" Curtis, a starter on the 1969–70 freshman team who had been an all-state player in his home state of Florida and had turned down many dozens of offers from other parts of the country in favor of traveling west.

The coaching staff liked both Curtis and Lee, but each had assets the other did not. Curtis was a fine ball handler, could shoot well, and was quick and fast, but he was weaker on defense than Greg. Lee had "quick" hands but couldn't match Tommy in running ability. He made up for this in part with his defense and persistence. Wooden said, "Never having been too quick or too fast, he must make up for this by intelligent play and has both the mental ability and basketball background to do this."

By any yardstick, though, it was a roster loaded with talent. The fierce competition for most of the positions helped keep interest and desire at a fever pitch as the conditioning activities brought everyone to a peak of physical excellence. Long before the season began, word was out that UCLA had another superteam in the making. The preseason polls all put the Bruins at the top of the mountain.

John Wooden tried to temper that. He had good arguments, he thought, why his fantastic period of NCAA domination might be over. Several weeks before the first game he said, "Logically speaking, the team is too young to win it all. But that doesn't mean I'm giving up. I never thought we'd win five in a row, or even four." And again: "There really hasn't been anything surprising or disappointing. I know the team is so young and I constantly have to remind myself of that fact. Last year's front line outweighed this year's by forty pounds. It was also three years older per man. Wilkes, for example, won't be nineteen until May, and Walton turned nineteen last Saturday. We are young, and youth tends to play more with emotion than reason. That's our problem."

Most observers took these statements with more

than a grain of salt. Doug Krikerian of the Los Angeles *Herald Examiner* wrote:

> You listen to John and you'd never realize that Bill Walton was the most dominant prep player ever to come out of San Diego, that other newcomers like Greg Lee, Tommy Curtis, Keith Wilkes, Vince Carson and Gary Franklin were all this and all that in high school and Henry Bibby may be one of the premier guards in the country and that youngsters like Sven Nater and Larry Hollyfield would be starting on most other teams.

As might be expected from all this, excitement and curiosity about the new Bruin edition swept far beyond the campus. It had never been easy to get tickets to Pauley when the Alcindor years got under way, but it was even harder to do as the Walton-led team moved into the spotlight. Many fans who couldn't get tickets to important home games were happy to get in to see the varsity preview with Nater anchoring one part of the varsity and Bill the other. The B team broke on top first as Nater got the tip and Greg Lee sank a shot soon after. The lead seesawed for a little while, but Walton's squad soon took over, winning easily, 86–54. Bill scored only 7 points, but he cleared 15 rebounds and started the fast break time after time with whistling outlet passes.

The first official test of the team was set for six days afterward, on December 3, 1971, when the Citadel College had the unenviable task of being initial guinea

67

pig. Citadel didn't figure to win; the main question was how well Walton and his supporting cast would do. Reporters from all parts of the country joined the noisy, exuberant UCLA crowd to see if the young team was as good as its early press clippings.

When the ball went up at center court at 8 P.M., the crowd let loose a tremendous wall of sound, a release of energy and anticipation that had been building for weeks. Walton soared high and controlled the tip. The crowd urged the team on and applauded and waved banners moments later when Bibby took a pass from Walton 20 feet out and let loose a perfect arcing shot that swished cleanly through the cords at 19:50 of the first half. The Walton Gang was off and running. It was the beginning of a deluge. Walton, Wilkes and the others choked off each Citadel attempt quickly and turned to the attack. Wilkes fed Lee who sank a 20 footer. He passed to Bibby who clicked from 17 feet out. For the first three and a half minutes, Bill was satisfied to pass off and pay defense. Then he took a pass deep in Citadel territory, turned to sink a two-pointer, and was fouled as he did so, setting up the first of many Walton three-point plays. At the half, UCLA led by 53–27. Long before the game ended, the subs were in, and the final tally was 105–49.

George Hil, the Citadel coach, dolefully gave the post-mortem to reporters. "They were awesome as usual. I think that this UCLA team compares with the first team from the Alcindor era. We tried to slow up the tempo, but with them dominating the boards, we couldn't play our game. In scouting reports, the word 'awesome' kept coming up all the time. If anything, it was an understatement."

The word went out on the wires: "No doubt about it, UCLA is good, very good." The team figured to move through the early part of its schedule without too much trouble, the first stiff test possibly coming from an experienced Ohio State team in the Christmas invitation tournament, the Bruin Classic. On the way to that confrontation UCLA proved steadily more devastating. The scores were astronomical—106–72 over Iowa, 110–81 over Iowa State, 117–55 over Texas A&M. Notre Dame was the school that had given UCLA its only loss the year before. Since then UCLA had chalked up 19 straight wins without a loss, and this time it was no contest. Notre Dame, weakened by graduation, fell in the first of a home-and-home series, 114–56. UCLA then whipped TCU and, in the first game of the Bruin Classic, the Univerity of Texas. Then it was ready to face Ohio State in the finals.

The Buckeyes featured All-Big-Ten guard Alan Hornyak, rated by many observers as a possible All-America candidate, and had a taller center than Walton in seven-foot Luke Witte. The odds still favored UCLA, but many writers from the Midwest expressed optimism that Ohio State would give the Bruins a tough battle and maybe even score an upset. Certainly, when the Buckeyes took warm-up practice, they looked strong and versatile.

Once the opening whistle sounded, though, Walton took full charge. While his teammates hounded and frustrated the offensive sallies of Ohio State, sometimes

69

forcing wild passes and other turnovers, Bill hovered in the backcourt behind Witte. As soon as Luke got a pass, Walton was on him, denying him the baseline and forcing him to start his moves farther from the basket than he was used to. In the first few minutes, the massive Witte went up for a shot, but the shorter Walton sprang above him by a foot or more to knock the ball away almost as if Witte were a forward. Minutes later Witte tried from another angle with the same result. It was obvious he was outmatched; he could do nothing against the swarming Bruin center. Bill's tactics picked up some personal fouls, but Witte was all but immobilized as Bill blocked six of his tries in the first fifteen minutes. Just after this, Walton had to turn things over to Nater when he drew a third foul, but by then UCLA had Ohio State on the run.

When it was over, Walton had only 10 points, but he had grabbed 12 rebounds, and his defensive efforts, as an awed reporter noted, "turned the Buckeye to jelly." He had help, of course; the Bruin floor men held Hornyak to just 10 points, most of those late in the game, his lowest ever, and UCLA finished ahead, 79–53. UCLA remained number one in the national polls, and most coaches felt it would stay there in the NCAA finals.

There were a few voices of caution. Walton and his mates had looked great up to that point, but all the games were at home. It remained to be seen how the inexperienced Bruins would react to the pressure of hostile crowds and unfamiliar playing conditions. The very next game was at the old, tension-packed field

70

house of Oregon State University where the jammed seats came down so close to the floor that the howling partisan audience almost seemed like a physical force for the Wooden squad to contend with. But Oregon State had more than that—a veteran team with a dazzling playmaker and set shot artist leading it named Freddy Boyd.

For a time it did not seem it would make much difference. The crowd screamed and yelled support for its favorites and hooted what it felt were unfair calls by the referees. Even though Walton was playing with an annoying cold and strep throat, he staved off many Oregon State sallies with blocks, steals, and pinpoint direction of the other Bruins. His rebounding and outlet passes sparked the fast break to a steady tattoo of field goals. By half time, UCLA led by 51–34, seemingly on the way to another 100-point-plus conquest.

But Oregon State came out in the second half with new spirit and a rugged hand-checking man-to-man defense. The roars of the fans redoubled, and the pressure seemed to get to the mighty Bruins. At one time or another Lee and Curtis made bad passes, Walton made some defensive errors, and even Henry Bibby made unexpected turnovers. At the same time Fred Boyd began to pick apart the UCLA defense with a string of sizzling shots from all sides. His efforts were aided by improved rebounding by center Neal Jurgenson and six six forward Sam Whitehead. OSU steadily narrowed the gap until with a little more than two mintes to go, UCLA was fighting for its life. Boyd hit to bring OSC within 7 points at 74–67. After a furious

71

battle around the boards, Walton sank what proved to be a vital score to make it 76–67. Jurgenson came right back with a basket, and it was 76–69. There was under a minute to go, and all UCLA had to do was hold the ball, but a steal brought Boyd sweeping in for a lay-up attempt which drew a foul from Hollyfield before the shot. Freddy hit one, missed the second, but Whitehead tapped the rebound in to make it 76–72 with thirty-two seconds left. The crowd was in a frenzy; there was still time for OSU to scramble back. Then the tension seemed to catch up with OSU too. In the final half minute both clubs made mistakes, turnovers; both missed shots until Greg Lee sank a two-pointer almost at the buzzer for a final 78–72 decision.

It was a close call, but it seemed to mature UCLA. From then on Walton and the others demonstrated confidence and poise almost every minute of every regular season game. UCLA moved from Corvallis to the even more menacing Macarthur Gym at Oregon University the next night and routed the Beavers. In game after game, as the season went by, UCLA almost seemed to toy with the opposition. Even USC could do little to stop them. After one such trying evening Stanford coach Howie Dallmar, third only to John Wooden and Kentucky coach Adolph Rupp in total career wins at the time, moaned, "Walton, he's the guy who did it. He destroyed us. He's the best big guy inside I ever saw. Yes, I'm saying he's better at this stage of his career than [Bill] Russell. He does things Alcindor never did." That evening, one in which Bibby scored 32 points, Big Bill had made 15 of 18 shots, scoring 32 points in twenty-eight minutes' playing time and taking down 15 rebounds.

Already Pac-8 champs, UCLA relaxed a bit, but still beat off a strong USC challenge in the last game, 79–66, to wind up an unbeaten regular season. Walton and company arrived at the NCAA regionals in Provo, Utah, odds-on favorites to win John Wooden a sixth straight and Walton a first national crown. The team did nothing to disprove that. With Walton, Bibby, Wilkes, and the rest showing their usual mastery of the game, they routed Weber State, 90–58, and Cal State Long Beach, 73–57. Watching Walton run through his repertoire of eye-popping maneuvers, a radio announcer, looking ahead to the finals at the Los Angeles Sports Arena on March 23 and 25, said, "If UCLA loses a game in this tournament, then Pat Paulsen will be elected President."

On paper it didn't promise to be that easy. There were strong contenders for UCLA to consider, beginning with a well-balanced University of Louisville team with a superguard named Jim Price whom many pro scouts rated a number one draft pick. And Louisville coach Denny Crum, fresh from many years as a Wooden assistant, was thoroughly versed in UCLA tactics. If Walton brought the team past that game, there was likely to remain Florida State, tall and rangy with two six eleven starters in a front line that had an overall weight and height advantage.

And Louisville did give the Bruins a fight for a while. Jim Price lived up to his press clippings, hitting long outside shots, jump shots from the key, running the team well and birddogging Bibby so tightly Henry rarely got a shot away. But Walton and the others picked up the slack. After a first half in which Louisville tied the score several times, UCLA drew steadily away in the second twenty minutes for a 96–77 triumph. Walton's contribution: 33 points, 21 rebounds.

Denny Crum told reporters, "This is the best UCLA team I've ever seen. They give you so many problems, and Bill Walton is amazing. He is awfully good and can do some different things that Lew didn't do. . . . We wanted to keep the ball away from him, but he gets to his spot on either side of the line fast. And he has such long arms and jumps so well. He gives you more problems than the average center I've seen. One thing that goes unnoticed is that he's smart. He's always in the right place, and he's always talking to his teammates so they'll be in the right place. He's a great leader."

Could Florida State win? "If they beat their press, keep the ball away from Walton [laughter] and shoot a good fifty percent of their shots."

When the capacity crowd got into the spirit of things two nights later, Florida State showed it might just meet those requirements. With two of its big men double-teaming Walton, they cut his effectiveness in the early going. At the other end, six eleven Lawrence McCray used his muscular frame to get position for some good inside shots, while six four Ron King peppered away from the corner. Florida State moved in front at the start and kept adding points until it had a 21–14 lead at the eight-minute mark, and the partisan UCLA

74

crowd was starting to worry. Some of the many writers pounding typewriters in press row wondered aloud if the pressure at the pinnacle might have finally thrown the young Walton Gang off stride.

But then the Bruins settled down and made the necessary adjustments to compensate for Florida State strategy. Walton brought his superior speed and quickness into play and threw extra effort into beating his rivals into position to control board play. He demonstrated his phenomenal leaping ability several times, seeming to rise a foot or more higher than usual to knock away a Florida State shot savagely. Wilkes, Bibby, and Tommy Curtis pitched in with a string of outside shots and a stifling defense. To rousing shouts of encouragement from the packed arena, UCLA made up the the early deficit and forged in front, forcing the increasingly panicky opponents into a string of turnovers. At half time the score was 50–39, and reporters were beginning to think about UCLA victory headlines.

However, Florida State regrouped and came out determined to make a game of it. UCLA kept scoring a reasonable part of the time, but the Seminoles from Tallahassee kept pecking away, and the increased tempo had its effect on frenzied play under the boards that caused Walton to pick up fouls.

With a lot of time left in the game the audience groaned as Bill drew his fourth foul and Sven Nater had to take his place. As Nater had done several times in the season, he battled fiercely and well for his share of rebounds. But Florida State had new confidence and momentum; with five minutes to go the UCLA lead dwindled to 79–72. Wooden put Greg Lee in for Tommy Curtis to work a stall game and run down the clock. The goal was for UCLA to try only high percentage shots and keep down the Seminoles' scoring opportunities. The plan worked. Florida State forced some turnovers and kept within striking range but never could get a rush going. The Bruins got some points to keep ahead, and then the clock wound down to where it was safe to return Walton to the lineup to restore full advantage to the Bruins' game. When the final buzzer sounded, the crowd gave a standing ovation to the hometown favorites' 81–76 victory.

Most of the team cheered, slapped hands, and grinned broadly. Henry Bibby was hoisted atop Sven Nater's shoulders to cut down one of the baskets for a souvenir. Walton shared in congratulations for a time but later made a statement to an interviewer that underlined his sometimes enigmatic personality: "I'm not elated at all. I don't even feel like we won. . . . Florida State is an excellent team, but we didn't play that well. We don't like to back into anything and in a way, I think that's what we did. . . ."

The other coaches and the writers hardly shared such doubts. To no one's surprise Walton was voted Most Valuable Player of the tournament. Against Florida State, he supplemented Bibby's 18 points, Wilkes' 23, and Curtis' 8 with the high point team total of 24. Besides scoring well, he collected 20 rebounds and made four shot blocks.

There was nothing backward about his season stats either. For the year as a whole he scored 633 points for an average of 21.1 a game. In field goals he sank 238 of 372 attempts for a 63.9 percent average and made 157 of 223 fouls for a 70.4 percent level. His 466 rebounds works out to 15.5 a game, figures that exactly parallel the sophomore record of Lew Alcindor.

6 Two in a Row

Now that the sensational 1971–72 season was behind him, Bill was a national celebrity. The added
publicity made him more uncomfortable than ever. He
discouraged intrusions in his private life and doggedly
tried to follow a normal routine. He gave first priority
to his studies. (After the NCAA tournament he and
Keith Wilkes were overwhelming choices for first-team
basketball All-Americans. They also were named to
the sports academic All-America roster for the first of
the three such honors.) After that he devoted his en-
ergies to such other pursuits as camping and political
involvement.

On campus Bill, like many college students if unlike
many athletes, was a champion of "liberal" causes. He
was especially outspoken about the Vietnam War,
which he vehemently opposed. He took part in rallies
and demonstrations against various aspects of that
American (and Vietnamese) tragedy, including one
that brought his views to national attention. The event
was a UCLA student sitdown strike on the major Los

Angeles artery of Wilshire Boulevard in protest against President Nixon's decision to send troops into Cambodia. The police came and dragged away the students, including Walton. He pleaded no contest when the case came up in court and was fined fifty dollars.

It was distressing to some Americans that Bill took parts in such activities, but the majority opinion probably was in his favor. The nation was disenchanted with the long and costly war. Besides, Walton's action was not strange for a student in those turbulent years. The reaction might have been quite different if some of Bill's views on the "system" had been published then. But at the time he was not giving many interviews, even about basketball.

The low profile he sought to establish did nothing to discourage rumors that kept showing up in the national media about his turning professional. Just his heroics of his sophomore year made him a strong candidate for offers of more than $1,000,000. The pros had developed a "hardship" category to justify signing college undergraduates which had brought lucrative long-term contracts to people like onetime Marquette center Jim Chones and Olympic star Spencer Hayward. Theoretically Bill also qualified. His family wasn't poor, but it was far from wealthy. If Walton accepted a huge bonus to sign with the National Basketball Association or American Basketball Association, his financial security was assured.

Though normally he could expect an equally good package in a few years, the argument could be made that something might happen to change the situation.

The most obvious would be an injury that could cut short his career. Or his playing might taper off, making pro teams less anxious to obligate themselves for large sums of money in advance.

The stories made good copy and continued to run, even though Bill had indicated his disinterest to reporters during the season. For example, when one interviewer queried him about it during a road trip early in 1972, Walton had taken out his wallet and extracted a singe dollar bill. "This is all the money I'm carrying right now," he said, indicating that was plenty for his immediate needs.

"They've called my parents and my brother because I don't have a phone and don't want to be bothered, but I've told them to refer everybody to Sam Gilbert. . . . Playing pro ball doesn't mean that much to me right now. I still need to improve my game right now. There are things I've got to work on—and I'm sure I'll be much better next year . . . besides, I think I'd be better off financially if I waited until I'm through playing college ball. I'll be a lot better player."

Many qualified observers agreed with the reasoning. Some suggested Bill wasn't ready emotionally to make the jump to the rough-and-tumble world of the pros at that time. For instance, the famed Lakers superstar Jerry West had discussed it at a sports luncheon shortly before the 1971–72 season ended. "Walton is the most overwhelming college sophomore I've ever seen." He stated he didn't think Bill would make it in the pros at that stage. "He needs college time to [learn] to survive the physical rigors and emotional demands of the pro 'meat grinder.' " But Walton had great potential. "He matches Russell in the art of the soul-crushing block. We've yet to see if he can match the stamina and strength of Chamberlain and the scoring of Jabbar. But Walton could be the first to combine the weapons of all the celebrated giants of the game in one person."

Though UCLA officials may have worried a bit, Walton himself ignored the whole matter during his vacation months, spending the summer as he pleased. He did the things that mattered to him far more than money or athletic stardom. He backpacked into remote wilderness areas by himself or with close friends, went on bicycle trips and in general tried to avoid urban areas where crowds might recognize him. In the fall he laid the speculation to rest by showing up on time for registration and, a few weeks later, for the first practice sessions of the new season.

It seemed certain to be a good year. Bill had a year of varsity play to his credit with all that meant in self-confidence, poise, and polish. His height had topped out at six eleven, but he had filled out from 210 to 220 or 225 pounds. No one had pushed him around the year before, but with the added muscular strength he promised to be an even tougher man to divert from his desired positions near the basket.

Of the superteam of the year past, only one starter was lost through graduation, Henry Bibby. He was a great player, but UCLA had two superb ball handlers back in Lee and Curtis. Lee had been the starting guard in 1971–72, with Curtis coming off the bench to provide capable replacement. Often Tommy had been a dynamic catalyst to regenerate a UCLA attack that had grown a bit sluggish. But competition between the two for a starter's role was fierce, if friendly, and it was possible Tommy would reverse the pattern in the new year. For the other guard spot, the Bruins had Larry Hollyfield, who had shown many moments of brilliance playing either guard or forward as a swing man. He displayed speed, amazing leaping ability, and fierce desire which made him powerful on the floor or under the boards.

At the forwards, Walton was flanked by the high scoring duo of Keith Wilkes and Lary Farmer. In pre-season analysis most experts picked Wilkes as an almost certain All-America along with Walton. Not only was he a scoring threat from all part of the court, but he was tenacious on defense, and his average of 8.2 rebounds a game the year before was second only to Walton on UCLA. For 1972–73, Wooden noted, "Keith seems a little heavier and stronger, which should help him in the physical contact under the basket at each end. He not only has great physical attributes but is an ideal youngster to have on your team in every respect. His play is so smooth, that it is often unappreciated by many." Farmer, the team's number four scorer in 1971–72, was also heavier and stronger without losing any of his speed and catlike reflexes.

Contributing to the phenomenal depth of the squad was Sven Nater, back for a second year as probably the best backup center in college ball. Two highly promising sophomores also played effectively in the three-and-three and five-on-five practice scrimmages, six seven forward Dave Meyers and swing man Pete Trgovich.

Coming into the new season, UCLA was now a proved, veteran team. No one wondered, as happened a year earlier, if they might be tripped up on the way to the title by inexperience. Every poll listed the team number one. It was an almost unanimous prediction that when the next March rolled around, Bill Walton would be facing some extremely talented but hapless center in the NCAA finals. Barring a miracle, observers agreed, John Wooden would have his seventh straight national title. Of course, no one would forecast that the team could go through 30 straight as in 1971–72. The law of averages indicated at least one loss might be in the cards; after all, it had happened to Acindor teams on a couple of occasions. The main question was whether that likely stumble would take place during the regular season or in the sudden-death play-offs. But if UCLA did win all its games, it would smash by a large margin the old all-time winning streak record set in the mid-fifties by the University of San Francisco.

Although UCLA had stars galore, few reporters paid much attention to anyone but Walton. Keeping in character, Walton said little for publication. He went about his business, sharpening his skills and encouraging his teammates in practice to do better. Those who played with him or were close to him in school claimed he was far from an introvert. He talked a lot about many subjects and enjoyed swapping stories and jokes. But on a public basis, he was practically a sphinx. Still, articles about him and his talents and habits filled countless columns in papers and magazines as the new series of intercollegiate basketball jousts got under way.

Some writers took note of his austere approach to life and his nonconformist attitudes. This was revealed in statements, infuriating to some, that he could see that blacks had good reason to hate whites and he did not blame them for it. Bill's ideas on grooming differed considerably from that of UCLA's coaching staff. That gave rise to rumors he might stage a confrontation with Wooden and his assistants about the requirements on hair length. For the most part, however, his image for most of the public and certainly with UCLA fans remained almost god-like.

The situation was summed up in his usual tongue-in-cheek manner by nationally syndicated Los Angeles *Times* columnist Jim Murray:

> The first thing you notice about William Theodore Walton, the deity of basketball, is that he's not a person, he's a belief. A religion. A bit of folklore. A legend before his own time.
>
> He doesn't have fans, he has disciples. The stories about him are not news, they're parables. You expect the heavens to part and the earth to tremble when he walks on court. You wonder why the other guys have the audacity not to salaam. . . .You're surprised he has to walk on

court. He should float on—like Peter Pan or Tinker Bell or the Angel Gabriel. . . .
You're suspicious of those long arms. Are they arms or electrodes? Do they bleed, or do they just unscrew at the shoulder? Are those eyes or tubes? Is the hair real, or dyed red plastics? . . . Since I saw Alcindor . . . and Chamberlain and Russell, and Oscar, and Elgin, and Jerry, I went out to check this living (?) legend the other night. . . .

First of all, he DOESN'T score every time he gets the basketball. He DOESN'T get every rebound. He DOESN'T score in double figures before he gets out of the dressing room. He needs a haircut. He DOESN'T make the other center disappear in mid-air in the middle of the game. He looks quite mortal—even clumsy at times. He DOESN'T play with the aloof, contemptuous superiority of a Jabbar, or the bored nonchalance of a Chamberlain, or the wicked intelligence of a Russell. The effort is obvious in his case. He's quite mortal, this young man. And quite vulnerable, actually. . . .

There was no doubt that some of Walton's impact on other teams was psychological, and many coaches tried hard to convince their players they could handle Walton and the Bruins if they really believed in themselves. But as the 1972–73 season unwound, there wasn't much evidence this was accomplishing much. UCLA started off against the University of Wisconsin at Pauley Pavilion on November 25, 1972, the way it had left off in March. Walton dominated from the opening jump ball, hitting a dazzling variety of shots and grabbing almost every loose ball that bounced off the plexiglass backboards. He received the usual standing ovation from UCLA rooters when he left the game for the usual ice pack treatment with a game high point total of 26 and a rebound count of 20.

The Bruins didn't seem likely to be tested until Christmas vacation, when they would travel to New Orleans to take part in the Sugar Bowl Classic. Nor were they as they breezed through five straight opponents with relative ease to bring their winning streak total to 51 games. For Bill Walton it had been a long time since he tasted defeat. Including the 49 straight of his Helix High career, the fifty-first win over the longtime UCLA nemesis Notre Dame, his quintets had won 100 games without a loss. Against the Irish, improving under Digger Phelps, but still below par, Bill had a relatively poor night, for him, of 12 points and 12 rebounds. But Wilkes, Hollyfield, and Curtis all were in double figures as the Bruins won going away, 82–57.

It was obvious by then, though, that things would be tougher for Wooden's team than in the last campaign. Coaches had closely analyzed the UCLA play of 1971–72 and had devised some new offensive and defensive tactics. More to the point, other schools had intensified recruiting, and many had vastly improved teams. Thus UCLA's scores had not topped 100 at all by the time the squad went to New Orleans in late December for the Sugar Bowl tournament. But Walton and the rest had also sharpened their defensive play, and opposing scores tended to be lower. The end result seemed to be the same, at any rate: UCLA went right on winning.

In the New Orleans invitation meet, however, the Bruins found themselves under fire. Drake put up a stalwart struggle before bowing by 85–72. Walton showed why he had led his team to a championship with one of his best nights ever, 29 points and 14 rebounds. Illinois, in the final game, used a deliberate style of offense that severely tested the Westwood five. The Big Ten representative hand-checked well and showed good outside shooting to keep right on UCLA's heels as the minutes went by. But Walton displayed his usual poise and determination, strongly aided by Farmer and Wilkes, rallying the Bruins again and again when it seemed the Illini might forge ahead. When the final buzzer sounded, UCLA had a hard-won 71–64 victory. Walton had scored 22 points and grabbed 16 rebounds, Wilkes had 16 points and 8 rebounds, and Farmer was outstanding, with 19 points and 10 boards.

All this, Coach Wooden stressed, was prologue. The heart of the season, he always pointed out, was conference play, because this was important not only in itself, but as the deciding factor for tournament selection. USC particularly had a talented, well-balanced, experienced team that could stifle the Bruins' title hopes if Bob Boyd's squad could achieve upsets in the two games between the teams.

Walton and UCLA expected to see more slowdown tactics as other teams tried to derail their blistering fast break, and it showed up in their first conference game against Oregon. The Ducks normally played a deliberate game, and they did even more so in the conference opener for both teams. It troubled UCLA and held their point total down. But the zone press caused Oregon turnovers, and Walton's presence in the middle ensured that the Ducks wouldn't get many points. Bill scored only 6 points, but he controlled the boards with 13 rebounds as the Bruins finished on top by 64–38. UCLA followed with three more wins over conference foes by sizable margins for a 4–0 record. USC kept pace, looking toward a key meeting in February after UCLA had whetted its skills against four non-conference foes: University of San Francisco, Providence, Loyola of Chicago, and Notre Dame.

Those four stood between UCLA and a new all-time winning record, and on paper, all had good enough personnel to score an upset. USF and Providence in particular looked good. The Dons had a tall front line with a mobile center in six six Kevin Restani, while Providence had a fine center in Marvin Barnes and a small, hot-shooting guard, Ernie Di Gregorio. But Walton gave devastating performances in all four games, getting more than 20 rebounds in all but the Notre Dame game, when he pulled down "only" 15, and scoring, respectively, 22, 18, 32, and 16 points. Larry Famer was a stellar player in all four, scoring in double figures in all but the Loyola game, while Keith Wilkes showed his consistent form with 13-, 17-, 16- and 20-point games.

Next came the Trojans at the Sports Arena, and a

turnaway crowd showed up to witness what everyone agreed might be the key game to both teams' season. To nobody's surprise USC went right into an unorthodox game plan. Oregon's Dick Harter said earlier when asked if a team could beat Walton and UCLA with a normal game, "There may be a team somewhere that can do it. But it's not in this conference." So USC began by conceding even the center jump. Center Mike Westra just stepped back so the Bruins would have to take the ball out of bounds, thwarting their chance for a fast break.

USC threw up a special collapsing defense against Walton and, when it got the ball, worked it back and forth in the forecourt, with the guards sometimes holding the ball motionless until the UCLA man came up to challenge. There were mingled cheers and boos from opposite sides of the court as the moments dragged on and the score sounded more like a baseball game than basketball. Every now and then the USC passing routine managed to spring forward Clint Chapman for a high-percentage jump shot from the foul line, and the score mounted slowly and evenly. Minutes went by, and it was 6–6, then 12–12 just past the ten-minute mark in the first half. Walton by then had scored only one point. Many in the audience remembered very well how a similar approach had brought a rare defeat to an Alcindor-led Bruin team, 46–44.

But then Walton broke loose, faked a USC defender beautifully to one side, and sprang high in the air, his hands a foot above the basket. The ball came right to him, and he dropped it gently into the net to put

UCLA in front, 14–12. The UCLA defense grew tougher, forcing USC to make wild passes that went out of bounds. Onlookers could sense the momentum was changing as Hollyfield charged through for a basket, 16–12. USC, obviously harried, was having trouble getting the ball out of the backcourt, and Walton was starting to make his presence felt underneath the baskets. Keith Wilkes hit an outside shot to make it 18–12. Moments later USC missed a shot, and Greg Lee fired one in from long range, 20–12. The Bruins soon worked a fast break, and Hollyfield made it 22–12. USC brought the ball in but couldn't get it over midcourt in the ten seconds allowed another turnover. Hollyfield let one fly that bounced off the rim, but there was Walton springing on high to guide the ball back down for the twelfth straight point without a USC answer.

That was the game. From then on USC had to try to play the normal run-and-shoot game favored by UCLA. Though USC was good, in a head-on challenge with the Walton Gang, it was no contest. UCLA won handily, 79–56, and Bill left to a thundering roar of approval with 4:55 left, having scored 20 points and claimed 17 rebounds. UCLA was now 5–0 and USC 4–1.

It wasn't all a romp after that. UCLA beat the Washington teams four straight for a 9–0 Pac 8 mark, but the team's fans had anxious moments watching the away games against Oregon and Oregon State on TV. Both those opponents played rugged, physical games with much pushing and elbowing for position.

Meanwhile, their fans added to the pressure with torrents of applause for their favorites and abuse for the visitors. In the first game UCLA built up a lead against Oregon, then had to fight doggedly to fend off Oregon charges. Sometimes the fighting almost took visible form as Hollyfield and an Oregon player exchanged words, and even Walton hotly told the Ducks' high-scoring Doug Little he was crowding too much.

In the end UCLA kept cool enough to defeat Oregon, 72–61. The next night Oregon State made UCLA work even harder. The Beavers used a stall game to good effect, tying the game on several occasions and never getting behind by more than a few baskets. But Walton was consistently winning the board battles and putting in enough points to make sure UCLA would come out on top, 73–67.

The next week UCLA beat California to clinch the Pac 8 crown. The main concern now was the NCAA classic, but UCLA till had two games left. The next one almost caught them napping. Stanford University, featuring seven-foot center Rich Kelly, threw another stall at the Bruins and did it so well they led by 7 points at the half, 28–18. With the home crowd screaming encouragement, though, the Bruins fought back in the second half to squeak through 51–45. Almost the entire UCLA team was shooting poorly, but Walton was the difference, putting in 23 points, almost half the team's total, and getting 10 rebounds. The squad reurned to form in the last game, vanquishing USC, 75–56, to complete a second straight all-winning regular season.

The pattern for the season seemed obvious. A slow-down could give UCLA trouble. Some experts thought at least one of the nation's best teams in the tournament might put everything together and end the Wooden hegemony. Arizona State, UCLA's first foe in the regionals, tried to run with them and were "blown out," 91–81. Wilkes scored 12 points, Holly-field his season high of 20, and Walton sank 28 points and accounted for 14 rebounds.

On paper the next game should have been easier. The opponent was the University of San Francisco, a team Walton and mates had manhandled two months before. But the USF coaching staff had gained new wisdom about possible ways of offsetting Bruin strength. Coach Bob Gaillard had schooled his team in a "controlled" offense in which the goal was not a full stall but rather a deliberate game with changing patterns of passing and cutting until a split-second lapse on UCLA's man-to-man defense might leave an opening for a high-percentage shot. USF's guards and its normally high-scoring, tall front-line man, center Kevin Restani (six nine) and forward Eric Fernsten (six eight) played with poise and great patience to make it work. On defense, the Dons fell back into a 2–3 collapsing zone with three big men surrounding Walton any time a play came his way.

The plan worked very well—for a while. With Restani on the baseline and Fernsten constantly working to get in position for jump shots from the foul line, USF gradually built up a lead. A little past the ten-minute mark, Restani made a flawless turnaround 10-

footer to give USF a 16–9 lead. But Wooden had adjusted by replacing Larry Hollyfield and Greg Lee with Tommy Curtis and Dave Meyers. After Restani's score the Bruins came to life with long-range outside shooting that is the key to beating a zone defense. While a tighter Bruin defense choked off USF scoring, Curtis hit one, two, three shots from 25 feet or more. Then Meyers came through with a jump shot, and UCLA led 17–16. Moments later Walton contributed by following a UCLA miss with a tip-in to make it 19–16. USF wasn't through yet. It took time and started scoring again. At half time UCLA held a slender 23–22 lead.

The two kept exchanging baskets at a slow tempo in the second half as USF stubbornly held to its strategy and kept UCLA from breaking it open. Within eight and a half minutes gone in the second half UCLA led by only 31–28. The key was controlling Walton. At times almost the entire USF team collapsed back on the Red Baron. But finally Bill found a little room. He came through with a soaring, lunging move to score on a follow shot, hustled back downcourt to foil a Restani shot and take the rebound. At 9:55 he outscrambled a trio of straining Dons to turn another Bruin miss into a tip-in two-pointer. The surge of activity finally rattled USF. Before they could settle down, the Bruins press got the ball back, and Curtis hit another long jumper. A minute later Larry Farmer scored, was fouled, and made the three-point play. UCLA led by 40–28, and USF never threatened after that.

Cal State Long Beach coach Jerry Tarkanian praised USF after UCLA walked off the court 54–39 winners. "You just can't play any better than USF did and still lose by fifteen points. But Walton, in a three-minute period, turned it around. He's amazing."

Now it was on to St. Louis for the finals. Of the four contenders, only UCLA had been a pretournament favorite. But Indiana, Providence, and Memphis State had shown great ability in beating higher-ranked teams. UCLA was overwhelming pick to win, but the other teams weren't going to be pushovers. Certainly Indiana, a young team with a future superstar in freshman guard Quinn Buckner, showed a courageous face. After scoring only 22 points in the first half, down by 18 points, Indiana fought back to within two points in the second half before Walton and his associates rallied to win, 70–59.

Once again UCLA was in the finals. This time it was unheralded Memphis State. An exciting team that had upset Denny Crum's Louisville squad to win the Missouri Valley Conference and an NCAA bid, the Tigers sported a six nine agile center in Larry "Dr. K" Kenon, and a flashy, slick ball-handling backcourt ace, six two "Little Tubby" Finch. Their supporting cast included tall, rugged scorers and rebounders such as six eight Rennie "Big Cat" Robinson, Bill "Billy Bipp" Buford, and six eight Wes Westfall. The team had fired the imagination of the hometown fans of Memphis, and a large percentage of the 19,301 fans crammed into the St. Louis Arena were rabid Memphis State rooters. When Walton and the others took practice, they were well aware they had no semblance of a home-court advantage.

Memphis coach Gene Bartow had said his team would run and shoot with UCLA. They tried, but even the height and speed of the well-honed Tiger team were no match for the Walton Gang on such terms. The Tigers played well and showed a good shooting touch, particularly Larry Finch who hit from all sides, but still UCLA kept edging ahead. Kenon played masterfully, but Walton kept blocking him out and brought cries of grudging admiration from the crowd as he showed masterful coordination in leaping skyward to grab soaring lob passes from Lee and Hollyfield which he swiftly converted into baskets. The effort of keeping up with Walton got Kenon into foul trouble early, and he had to sit down with 7:49 left in the half.

The Tigers went into a 1-2-2 zone and slowed down the pace. Doggedly they fought to keep the Bruins out of scoring range, then moved back on attack to score. UCLA got some points, but Memphis State got more. When the teams went off at half time, the partisan crowd roared approval of the 39–39 tie score. Walton picked up his third foul with 4:14 left in the period, but Wooden decided he couldn't afford to take Walton out in the seesaw contest.

In the second half Memphis State retained the zone and kept up the pressure. The game was still anyone's in the early minutes, and Memphis State twice got ahead with baskets from Kenon and Finch. But there was no stopping UCLA. The Walton Gang started picking the zone apart with outside shooting by Keith Wilkes and Lary Hollyfield and always those unstoppable Walton plays. The guards kept feeding him the ball from all over the court, and his ability to go up for the ball and place it in from an almost infinite number of angles seemed uncanny. And if Bill wasn't taking lob passes, he was tipping in rebounds of other players' attempts. Some of the baskets were fairly simple exercises, but many were spectacular. One such occurred midway through the period, when Walton came in from behind a play, seemed to stretch almost to the arena rafters as he brought his hand up—and back—to push a rebound whizzing toward the end line back behind him into the net.

Walton did most of this after drawing foul number four about seven and a half minutes into the second half. Wooden left him in, and the super redhead never slowed down a minute. Somehow he continued to dash from one end to the other, crash the boards with abandon, get off sizzling outlet passes without making the misstep that would bring the fifth foul and automatic ejection. The foe couldn't get him out, but a twisted ankle finally sidelined him with 2:51 remaining. By then, though, UCLA had the game won and coasted to a final margin of 87–66.

When it was over, the Walton Gang had won 60 straight, Wooden a seventh straight national title, and Bill was unanimously voted the Player of the Tournament. The statistics were almost unbelievable. Bill had garnered 13 rebounds, blocked a number of shots, and scored 44 points. He had tried 22 field goals, most of them on high lobs, and scored 21 of them. Lee, who had 14 assists, told a reporter, "When you've got a guy 6-11 and they don't have anybody on him, it's stupid not to go to him. . . . Bill and I have eye contact first. Sometimes I throw it. Sometimes I don't. . . . I throw it if he points up, but first I would hesitate, then look one way, then pass it when they weren't expecting it."

The Bruins were celebrating as soon as the game ended. Hollyfield and Farmer exchanged soul slap after soul slap while Nater, Meyers, Curtis, Lee, and Wilkes slapped each other's backs and raised their fingers in number one signs. Walton just sat on the bench as Wooden affectionately rumpled the curly red locks. Then, saying little, he limped toward the Memphis State bench. He liked to win, but he felt sympathy for the team that had dropped such a pressure-filled, hard-fought game. He found Larry Kenon, shook hands with him, and tried to cheer up the sad-faced Dr. K. As some reporters said in surprise, from outward appearances one would have thought Walton was on the losing rather than winning side.

But there was no doubt of whose side Bill was on for coach Bartow. "He's about as physical a big man as I've ever seen. He did so many things so well that we just couldn't stop him. He's super—the best collegiate player I've ever seen. We tried three or four things, but I guess we didn't try the right one, if you let him have the ball, he'll kill you."

7   The Streak

When the UCLA team closed out its second straight 30–0 season with the Memphis State victory, it had already assured itself a legendary place in the annals of basketball. The 60-straight wins of the Walton era added to the 15 games without a defeat of the 1970–71 team gave the Bruins the longest unbeaten string by far in the history of the college game. The feat easily eclipsed the previous record of 60 straight that had been set by the peerless University of San Francisco team of 1955–56–57 which had starred the great Bill Russell.

The 75 consecutive victories of UCLA far outpaced even the achievements of the Alcindor years. With Lew showing the way, UCLA had reached an impressive total of 47 in a row from February 25, 1966, to the famous two-point loss to Houston in the Astrodome on January 20, 1968. Until the Walton years that string ranked second only to USF's 60. After the Houston loss Alcindor helped the Bruins go another 41 in a row from January 26, 1968, to another two-point defeat—by USC on March 8, 1969. At the time the 41 string became the sixth longest win streak in college basketball history. But the Walton Gang's two unbeaten seasons in a row equaled the USF string by itself and was certain to surpass it in 1973–74 if Walton didn't succumb to the increasingly lucrative offers to turn pro.

The new superstreak began on January 30, 1971, when the Wickes-Rowe-Patterson-Bibby team rebounded from a loss one week earlier to Notre Dame, 89–82, with a 74–61 triumph over University of California at Santa Barbara. There were some close calls later in the season, but UCLA won them all on the way to the national title. The Red Baron had then come along to spark the new Wooden juggernaut. There wasn't much discussion in the sports pages of a possible new victory record during 1971–72 when many writers and coaches still expected the youthfulness of the Walton Gang to cause it to stumble at least once or twice in that season. Once Bill and friends had blitzed their way through 30 straight, getting more impressive almost every outing, many experts observed that only a miracle seemed likely to derail the Bruins, barring a critical injury to Walton.

As Bruin opponents continued to wind up on the short end of the score in 1972-73, the countdown began for the magic numbers—60 to tie and 61 for the new laurel. Some forecasters thought UCLA might have trouble winning number 58 against the team representing the school that held the record. But though USF was talented and fired up, it could do little to stop

UCLA's momentum. The win over Providence then set the stage for games 60 and 61. To add to the pressure on the Walton Gang, they had to travel to Chicago to face Loyola of Chicago, then move on to meet their old nemesis Notre Dame in the field house of South Bend, Indiana, where UCLA had lost its last game before the streak began.

The Loyola team, though a heavy underdog, played a strong game to try to halt the streak. UCLA, with Wilkes and Hollyfield hitting from outside and Walton doing his usual heroics around the basket, moved in front early and stayed there, but the Chicagoans scored too and trailed by only 47–39 at half. The story was much the same in the second period. UCLA never had an insurmountable lead, but Loyola could not mount a rush to close the gap. At the end UCLA had a hard-earned 87–73 decision. Wilkes had 16 points and an eye-catching 15 rebounds to his credit, and Hollyfield tallied 14. But the difference primarily could be seen in Walton's statistics: 32 points and a fantastic 27 rebounds, only one shy of the UCLA all-time record of 28 set by Willie Naulls.

A novelist could hardly have set the stage better for the Notre Dame rematch. Irish fans could sense the drama: basketball history would be made no matter which team won, and their team had been the only one to take UCLA's measure in three years. Every seat in the arena on the Notre Dame campus was taken, and tickets could easily have been sold to double the 11,343 on hand if there had been room. In tens of millions of homes all around the nation the

TV channel was set to the coast-to-coast telecast of one of the major events of the year and of sports annals in general.

Notre Dame had an excellent team with fine shooters and ball handlers in Gary Brokaw, Peter Crotty, and Dwight Clay and an All-American candidate in center forward John Shumate. But it was a squad UCLA had handled easily earlier in the year. On paper the Bruins had a sizable edge. However, Notre Dame was at home, with the usual highly charged crowd rooting for it. And the Irish had the precedent of stopping the previous UCLA victory march under similar circumstances.

The intensity of feeling on Notre Dame's players showed in their faces when the action began and in the close guarding they applied to the Bruins. Emotions ran high, and at times players almost came to blows. At one point Hollyfield and Crotty shoved each other. The boos from the crowd didn't disturb Larry. As he said later, elbows were being thrown, "and somebody hit him [Crotty] in the nose and he started crying. I just said, 'Get him out of here. He's crying.'" Walton and Shumate also battled furiously for position all over the court and the heat of battle got so high that the usually imperturbable coach Wooden went to the Notre Dame bench and warned Irish coach Digger Phelps he might put Nater in to even things up with Shumate physically.

Despite the high voltage atmosphere, UCLA refused to get rattled. It played its own game with what amounted to a controlled ruthlessness that blunted the

Notre Dame attack and systematically tore apart their defense. Wilkes, Farmer, Hollyfield, Lee, and Dave Meyers took turns peppering the Notre Dame basket with successful outside shots. When the Irish came out to try to take away the outside game, Walton went to work with lay-ups and tip-ins. Even when UCLA missed, its board work was peerless. On a few occasions, Walton, Wilkes, Hollyfield, and even the guards batted the ball around the basket three, four, or five times unti it finally went in.

UCLA scored first and steadily increased its lead to 38–25 at half. The Irish still weren't too far behind. But the Bruins started the second half with a barrage of shots that put them in front, 61–39, and all concerned knew it was over. The final score was 82–63, and no one could deny that UCLA was probably all-time number one. Walton scored 20 points and had 15 rebounds, while Farmer and Wilkes closed with 16 points each.

Coach Wooden, smiling broadly, obviously relished the new pinnacle. "I'm very happy about it," he told reporters, "but it doesn't compare with winning your first national championship. It's the continuation thing that makes you proud. It's not something one team could do all by itself."

Walton also was relaxed and affable. As usual, he stressed he was only a contributor, "It's an accomplishment for the team," he said to interviewers. "We like pressure, even though we haven't felt it too much. I know I thrive on it. And I like hostile crowds. They make me want to play better." But as far as the streak was concerned, he noted, "You've got to remember fifteen of those games came on the Wicks and Rowe team. I've only been a part of forty-six of them."

Phil Woolpert, who had coached the University of San Francisco team that had held the record for sixteen years, admitted he would have liked to keep the honor. "But I've been anticipating UCLA's breaking it for some time. In fact, when they reached forty-seven with this particular group of players. I figured it was just a matter of time. . . . UCLA is an extremely well-blanced team. Walton is their stickout, no question about it, but he has to have a great supporting cast as Russell had when he was in college.

"Any team has to have a dominating man—someone who makes the other team change its game. That's what Walton has done, and what Lew Alcinor did, and that's what Russell did."

But the streak would end sometime. "I don't know when or by whom. I don't see anyone on the immediate horizon. I'm sure that John feels the same way—that it will ony be a matter of time before they are beaten. And then they'll start another string."

The time, however, was not at hand. Every night a new opponent took the court with dreams of being the giant killer, but the weeks passed by, and all that happened was that UCLA added more games to the win column. When Walton led his team to the 1972–73 national title, there were really two unbeaten skeins still intact. In successive games, the total stood at 75 —and counting. But perhaps more astounding was UCLA's tournament streak of 36 in a row. Those 36

103

victories had been scored over the best teams in the nation under sudden-death conditions where a single off night meant season's end. For Bill Walton, the happy conclusion of 1973 meant he had played in 129 consecutive games in high school and college without ever knowing the bitter taste of defeat.

Despite coach Wooden's warning that even the greatest team could have an off night and his agreement with coach Woolpert that this would occur sooner or later, Bruin fans reviewing Walton's 1972–73 achievements found it hard to believe it could happen in 1973–74. Walton had been voted the nation's Player of the Year for the second straight year. He had scored 612 points for a two-year total of 1,245. In rebounding, his 506 for 1972–73 set a new UCLA season record. His two-season rebound mark of 1,072 exceeded Alcindor's statistic for the same period by 150.

UCLA figured to be overwhelming choice for number one in 1973–74, and that was the way all preseason polls came out. But there were some unbelievers, particularly from the Tarheel state of North Carolina. They cited the fact that a superb team, one that sported some sensational shooters and a burly seven-foot center had also gone undefeated in 1972–73: North Carolina State. That squad, the Wolfpack, had been ruled ineligible for NCAA tournament play because of recruiting violations. If the Wolfpack had confronted Walton and Company, things would have been different, Carolinians swore.

UCLA had taken up the challenge, though. A game between the schools was placed on the mid-December schedule. The Wolfpack stars were back, including the center, Tom Burleson, and human jumping jack David Thompson. Walton had once more ignored professional overtures, and the stage was set for a certain "game of the year" and possibly even the end of the streak.

A few analysts wondered, but not too loudly, whether the Bruins really would be as strong for Walton's last year. There seemed little loss in strength. Wilkes, Lee, and Curtis were back; Pete Trgovich and Dave Meyers figured to be a little stronger and much smoother players. There were fine prospects joining the squad, such as the broad-shouldered, hard-driving six five and a half freshman forward Marques Johnson and one of the most sought-after prep players of the previous year, six nine center forward Richard Washington, whom the governor of his home state of Oregon had called "a natural resource not for export." Additional support was promise by seven one sophomore center Ralph Drollinger and the ball-handling wizard from Philadelphia Andre McCarter.

The Bruins had suffered some serious losses through graduation, however. Sven Nater had gone, promptly showing just how good he was by becoming one of the top centers in the American Basketball Association. Drollinger was taller, but he didn't have the muscular build or the experience Nater had provided as Walton's backup man. Farmer and Hollyfield also had departed, and it remained to be seen whether their replacements could equal their drive and determination when the going got tough.

UCLA started out smartly, opening the season with a decisive win over Arkansas, number 76 in the streak. But then came Maryland. From the same conference as North Carolina State, Maryland featured a gifted center in Tom Macmillan and a fine, balanced team. They gave UCLA a spine-tingling struggle on the Bruins' home court at Pauley before bowing by a single point, 65–64. Looking ahead two weeks to North Carolina State, many experts shook their heads. Maryland was a first-rank team, and its good showing against Wooden's aggregation wasn't surprising. But North Carolina State was, if anything, better: conference champ over Maryland the year before and favorite to repeat in the new season.

After warming up against SMU on December 8, the Bruins went to St. Louis a week later for the showdown. The packed stadium of 19,000 was almost 100 percent for the underdog from Carolina and demonstrated it with earsplitting cheers as the Wolfpack ran through its practice routines. Burleson, Thompson, and watch-charm guard Monty Towe (five-four) looked sharp and confident as they whipped through their pregame warm-up.

Throughout the first half it was anybody's game. Towe hit with precision from the corners, and Burleson and Thompson added points here and there. But it was obvious that the East Coast giant was having his problems with the Red Baron. Walton boxed him out again and again and on more than one occasion caught him flat-footed with a deceptive move that cleared the way for an easy score. Wilkes, too, was doing his part, hounding Thompson so the six-four forward had to hurry his shots. Burleson's opposition was taking a toll, however.

Bill drew fouls and, when he reached four in the first half, had to sit down until well into the second period. Drollinger came off the bench and held his own as Walton shouted encouragement from the side-lines. It was still a horse race, with Carolina only a basket or two back, right up to the halfway mark of the second period. Then Walton returned and turned things around. He scored almost immediately and followed up with a dazzling display of basketball that made Carolina defenders commit a series of costly turnovers. Wilkes broke loose with one amazing shot after another, often deftly set up by a pass from Walton. Walton became even more dominating on the boards, and UCLA coasted to an 84–66 win for their seventy-ninth straight.

The win erased all the doubts of analysts. UCLA was still number one, and the forecasts were for a third glory year for Walton that would take the streak past 100 games. Certainly the Wolfpack contest seemed to mold the team into a high-powered unit. In the next game the Bruins routed a good Ohio University team, 110–63. Walton played only half the game, getting 15 rebounds and 13 points in that time. A win over St. Bonaventure served as tuneup for another Bruin Classic tournament, in which the Walton Gang trampled Wyoming, 86–58, then thrashed a Michigan University team in the finals that sported the sensational All-America forward Cazzie Russell by 90–70.

Eveything went well in the Pac-8 opener as UCLA traveled to Seattle to hand the University of Washington one of its worst losses in history, 100–48. The next game was one UCLA won, but paid for dearly.

Facing Washington State in Pullman, Washington, UCLA slowly ground out a growing lead against a stall by the Cougars and led 49–33 with about ten and a half minutes left. Then Dave Meyers, playing brilliantly at forward, directed a lob pass at Bill that Walton took in midair and whirled to try a lay-up. But Bill was off-balance and fell backward over the Cougars' reserve center Rick Steele. Walton flipped over Steele's crouching figure and hit the hardwood floor with a resounding smack. For moments the six-eleven form was motionless, and fear rippled through the Bruin players. But Walton stirred, then got up slowly, holding his back. He smiled, joked, and said he'd be all right. But when he went back into the game a few moments later, his back bothered him too much to continue. He went to the locker room, while UCLA went into a slowdown of its own that salvaged its eighty-fifth straight and forty-fifth conference win in a row.

The Walton injury at first was diagnosed as a bruise that wouldn't keep him out of the next contests. But it turned out more serious than predicted. He missed the next game against California, then didn't suit up for Stanford. People started wondering if he might miss the Notre Dame game coming up in South Bend on January 19. As usually happened, it shaped up as a crucial contest. The Irish had improved mightily over the year before, with John Shumate playing even more spectacularly and with new faces on hand such as the highly talented freshman Adrian Dantley. Without Walton UCLA might be outmanned, experts said.

Meanwhile, coach Wooden demonstrated his uncanny skill by getting extra effort from the other squad members. With Drollinger and Rich Washington taking over Walton's chores reasonably well and Meyers, Wilkes, Curtis, Lee, and the rest blending their abilities unselfishly, UCLA kept winning. None of the games was a runaway, but UCLA had no unusual difficulties in beating California, Stanford, and, in preparation for Notre Dame, the University of Iowa. Iowa, not a top-level team, fought hard before succumbing as the eighty-eighth consecutive victim in the UCLA victory march.

As UCLA moved on to South Bend, the big question was whether Walton would play and, if he did, would he be able to be in top form after a week and a half of inactivity. The anticipation of the nation's fans was, if anything, more intense than for the North Carolina State imbroglio. Over the years the UCLA-Irish games had become one of *the* traditional basketball rivalries. Even a weak Irish squad had often given Wooden-coached teams more than they bargained for —and this Irish quintet potentially was of national championship calibre.

At South Bend, Irish coach Dick "Digger" Phelps and members of the faculty and student leaders worked to build self-belief in the fans and team. At Saturday morning mass the day of the game, the Reverend Edmund F. Joyce, executive vice-president of the university, said, "This is not just an ordinary day. The chances are good that years from now you will look back on this day as one of the most memorable ones in your life. Is this melodramatic? I don't think so. . . ."

Digger Phelps told reporters, "If we can stay healthy . . . if we can stay out of foul trouble, it's going to be interesting. If we win, it'll be remembered in ten years that Notre Dame won." The key would be outscrapping the Walton Gang on the boards. Phelps noted his team didn't have anyone as tall as Walton, but it had a group of strong-armed, quick performers in six-nine Shumate, six-five Dantley, six-seven Gary Novak, and freshman reserve six-five Bill Paterno. In a physical, rough-and-tumble game, he indicated, they could hold their own with anyone.

"You can't beat UCLA with one shot at a time. You have to get second and third shots to win. We have to do a job on the boards. Particularly offensive rebounds. We're got to be physical."

Emotions were at a fever pitch when viewers turned on the nationally televised event that Saturday afternoon. Waves of students carrying banners that said such things as GOD MADE NOTRE DAME NO. 1 surged through the aisles, shouting and singing fight songs. Irish cheerleaders, including a student in traditional leprechaun garb, acrobatically led packed tiers of supporters in deafening yells, and ushers struggled to keep some of the weaving columns from getting in the way of the practicing athletes. If crowd pressure was a factor, the Irish had it made.

One sobering note had entered, however. Walton

was suited up and would play, though the fact that he had to wear a special corset for his back boded ill for him, considering Irish plans for an all-out backboard war.

But when action got under way, it didn't seem as if the injury or the layoff had done Walton too much harm. His moves were perhaps a bit rusty, but not enough to cut into his usual control of the boards. The Irish fought hard, with Dantley, Shumate, guard Dwight Clay, and others breaking the Bruins' zone press fairly easily. But once in Bruin territory, things got sticky. The Bruins guarded closely and well, and Walton more than held his own against one, two, or three Irish front-line men at a time. Notre Dame's deliberate style cut down on UCLA's scoring opportunities, but when Walton, Wilkes, Meyers, or Curtis got a shooting chance, he made the most of it. At half time UCLA had a sizable lead derived from a shooting percentage of 70 percent.

Notre Dame regrouped for the second half as the crowd redoubled its screams and applause, exhorting them to show the old Irish spirit and rally. Phelps changed his offensive and defensive patterns, but nothing seemed to work. The score remained in the Bruins' favor as the clock went past the halfway mark. The minutes ticked by as the teams battled back and forth, but every time the Irish scored, UCLA matched it, then often added an extra basket. The time wound down to six minutes to go, five minutes, four, and at 3:30, Phelps called time with the scoreboard showing

UCLA 70–Notre Dame 59. It seemed nothing could stop UCLA from claiming its eighty-ninth straight.

On the sidelines Phelps told the team they could still do it. "We've got to make some changes, and we can't quit now." He made a crucial adjustment. He took out the muscular Paterno and replaced him with another freshman, guard Ray Martin. Martin was a key element in the man-to-man pressing defense Phelps told the team to use. He theorized Martin's speed might pick up the tempo and make the press considerably more effective.

Phelps himself was surprised at how well the strategy worked. UCLA suddeny found difficulty in bringing the ball upcourt. Such usually dependable performers as Curtis and Wilkes started throwing the ball away. Each time Notre Dame took advantage, hitting with deadly accuracy from outside and even inside. The layoff may have got to Walton. He obviously was tiring and was just a step or two slower in getting back into position. As the roars of the crowd crescendoed, the miracle Phelps had prayed for took place. UCLA kept missing its shots, tried to go into a stall as Notre Dame crept inexorably closer, but nothing worked. In an unbelievable three minutes, the Irish closed the gap. Basket after basket went in until UCLA's lead was only 70–69 inside the one-minute mark.

A UCLA turnover gave Notre Dame the ball out of bounds. An assistant coach asked Phelps if he didn't want to call time-out to set up a special play. "No," he said, "we've got momentum going our way, let's keep it going. A time-out might kill our momentum."

The crowd was on its feet, yelling, shrieking, waving hands and banners as the Irish brought the ball down. The TV announcer theorized they might try for the last shot, but as they worked into position, no signal came from the bench. With twenty-nine seconds left, the ball was in the hands of Dwight Clay deep in the right-hand corner.

Clay didn't hesitate, He took aim and let fly a fall-away jumper over the desperately outstretched fingers of a Bruin defender. The ball seemed guided by unseen hands as it arced perfectly toward the basket, then hit the nets to an accompanying roar from the stands that made the walls vibrate. The Irish had outscored UCLA, 12–0, in three minutes time and led 71–70.

Wooden called time. Twenty-one seconds showed on the clock, and many a Bruin team had come from behind in past years under such circumstances. But this time the magic was gone. The Bruins made a run at it, but missed as the gymnasium broke loose in pandemonium. Hastily scribbled banners read GOD DID MAKE NOTRE DAME NUMBER ONE and thousands swirled all over the court, hoisting Dentley, Clay, Shumate, and others on their shoulders for a writhing, exuberant victory dance.

The streak was over in a setting that would have seemed improbable in a movie script. It had ended where it had begun some three years before. Notre Dame wins at South Bend bracketed UCLA's phenomenal achievement. Both the Irish highpoints and the Bruin streak would be a part of basketball legend evermore. The Notre Dame feat also brought an equally impressive string to a close, the 157 consecutive games Bill Walton had played in without a loss.

Phelps told a reporter he thought breaking the streak was "good for college basketball." To which Wooden responded "If so, then you'd have to say that having such a streak was bad for college basketball. I think this streak was the most tremendous thing there ever was for college basketball. Look at all the interest it generated and all the enthusiasm there was at Notre Dame before the game."

As for Walton, he seemed to take it in good grace. He didn't like losing, but there was always next week. In fact, there was another game with the Irish, but at Pauley Pavilion.

8 Near Miss at Greensboro

After the Notre Dame game the Bruins quietly washed and dressed, while shouts and taunts echoed through the corridor outside from triumphant Irish supporters. While the team waited for coach Wooden to come down from the courtside interviews with TV sportscasters, Walton consoled his teammates and blamed himself for the fall. He took no note of the fact that two quick steals from other UCLA players had started the Notre Dame resurgence. He had not done well enough on the boards, he said, grabbing only nine rebounds.

But then Wooden arrived and put things back in perspective. The coach analyzed some of the game circumstances in a calm, straightforward manner. He concluded his brief talk: "Now we've got to go out and break that long one-game losing streak."

On Monday, while UCLA went through its practice hours at home in Pauley, the polls came out, and as expected, both wire services showed Notre Dame number one. But despite the Irish' 10–0 record and the

UCLA shocker, more than a few writers and coaches refused to believe Notre Dame really was the reigning monarch on the basis of a single-point margin. In the AP poll, while thirty-six selectors gave the Irish their first place vote, 15—almost half as many—still gave the honor to the Walton Gang. If Notre Dame won the second game a week later at Pauley, they reasoned, they'd believe Walton's crew had met its match, but not before.

For as Wooden had said earlier in the season, "A lot of people probably will laugh at me when I say this, but I'm convinced there are a lot of teams that can beat us. However, I don't think they could beat us in a series of games—particularly if they were all on a neutral court."

One team that obviously made the mistake of catching the Walton Gang on the rebound was Santa Clara. In the "dress rehearsal" for the Irish rematch, the UCLA onslaught was brutal. Walton played with a seeming total disregard for his physical safety. He left his feet again and again in breathtaking swoops and leaps to control the flight of the tan sphere. Sometimes he hit the floor with a crunch that brought gasps from the crowd. But each time he was on his feet like a rubber ball, rushing swiftly back into the fray. There was little Santa Clara could do as UCLA thundered to a 96–54 victory as the crowd urged them on with shouts of "Beat Notre Dame! Beat Notre Dame!"

It seemed as though the Irish could hear footsteps, too. Traveling across county for the second game, Notre Dame stopped off for a match with the University of Kansas and, while UCLA was manhandling Santa Clara, the Irish barely edged the Jayhawks in a close, bitter battle. In the days that followed, as newspapers across the country printed forecasts, comments, and color stories on the big game participants, John Wooden drove his team through sweat-soaked practice sessions.

On Saturday night, January 26, TV cameras again focused on frenzied rooters and a kaleidoscope of noise and color. But this time the cheers were all for the Bruins in their home uniforms of white with blue and gold numbers and piping. There were a few rounds of applause and scattered yells when the Notre Dame squad in its bright-green road uniform with the shamrock in front were introduced.

As the UCLA cheerleaders formed a lane for the Bruin starters, the sounds arose in waves that reverberated from wall to wall, reaching a shattering sustained level when Big Bill ran onto the floor. He rushed out to join the other starters, a wicked grin on his face as he exchanged a series of soul slaps with them. The faces this time were a little different. Coach Wooden had shaken up his lineup. Dave Meyers remained on one wing, but Marques Johnson took over on the other side in place of Pete Trgovich to provide extra rebound strength and free Dave Meyers for more passing moves to Walton in the low post.

It took a few minutes for a pattern to develop. The crowd approved noisily when UCLA made the first two points, then roared even more lustily when Walton and his coworkers added another two—and two after that—with no response from the Irish. It was becoming apparent that Walton was up for this game and at his intimidating best, denying the Irish the middle while the other Bruins harassed them with the zone press and kept a hand in the face to disconcert any opponent who tried to get set for a field goal. UCLA made some mistakes. Walton walked a few times to lose sure scores, and some of the Bruin passes were a little off target. But UCLA made up for the relatively few lapses with a textbook-perfect smothering defense. As the scoreboard clock flashed the passing seconds, Notre Dame seemed to lose concentration, to show signs almost of panic. The Irish had blanked UCLA for three and a half minutes the week before, and the Walton Gang was returning the compliment by shutting out Notre Dame for an even longer time. At 14:30, with Notre Dame behind, 9–0, coach Phelps called time out to calm his team down, and moments later Adrian Dantley hit a jumper to make it 9–2.

The Irish regained a little composure, but while their play looked more organized, Walton was playing with controlled fury. Again and again Notre Dame worked the ball into UCLA territory, setting up an inside play for Big Shu, Dantley, or Brokaw, only to find the unsettling figure of Walton suddenly in view. The Irish forced their shots, taking most of them awkwardly off-balance and ended up out of position as the ball ricocheted into the hands of Walton, Wilkes, or Johnson. At the ten and one half minute mark, Notre Dame had taken fifteen shots and made only three. Still, they did manage to close to within 8 points, 19–11.

Then Big Bill led a typical UCLA breakaway. He took an arcing lob pass from Meyers, playing in the left-wing spot normally held by Trgovich, and guided it in. The next time on attack he went up with a classical sweeping hook over Shumate's straining hands. He showed still another move for his third straight basket as he let fly a successful push-type hook which the sweating Irish center could do nothing to stop. Keith Wilkes capped this surge with his trademark over-the-head jumper that made it 27–15.

At the end of the first half UCLA had a 33–17 margin. Walton had gone 7 for 7 for 14 points which, combined with Wilkes' 18, made up 99 percent of UCLA scoring. Only Shumate of the Irish was in double figures with 12.

Irish fans prayed for a comeback like that of a week before, but this time the luck of the Irish had evaporated. Walton kept up his sizzling performance with his eighth-straight field goal. Soon after, he brought the crowd to its feet as he picked off a rebound and got off a length-of-the-court pass to a speeding Tommy Curtis, who had to go only a few more steps for an unopposed score. Bill picked up fouls here and there and finally fouled out at 5:39, but by then the Bruin momentum was such that Notre Dame had no chance to recover. Bill loped off for his knee treatment to a torrent of applause, holding his finger high in the air in a number one sign. Walton had scored 32 points, picked off 11 rebounds, and ensured that come the next polls, UCLA would be on top again.

Wooden told reporters that feeding Walton on the

low post was a vital factor in the 94–75 verdict. "Dave Meyers is taller than Pete Trgovich, and he is able to see over the defenders a little better to make the pass into Bill. We have a tremendous scoring machine in Bill, and until somebody stops him, we should try to get the ball into him."

UCLA and Walton had proved once more that when they were fired up for a game, they were an irresistible force. But they continued to show puzzling lapses. Right after the display of outstanding basketball against the Irish, the team came close to beating itself with costly mistakes against crosstown foe USC.

Wooden told reporters the team was more impatient than the year before and not as coachable. It was, perhaps, senioritis. "When they all were sophomores, I told them all their eagerness, attentiveness, and response to what I was trying to get across made them one of the finest groups of youngsters I've ever coached. I also told them, however, that by the time they were juniors they would not be quite as responsive and that when they were seniors they would be intolerable in this regard—but not mean to be.

"Mainly it's a matter of telling them something and they nod 'yes' and they do exactly what you don't want them to do. There were a couple of times one game when we told them during a time out to change to the full-court press, but the adjustment was not made. In other words, we get lip service—they listen but do not hear."

Still, the Red Baron always seemed able to get the team to rise to the occasion when the stakes were high.

Right after the USC close shave, Oregon came to Pauley tied for first, and the teams collided in a blistering body-checking, elbow-bumping battle where almost every other play seemed to bring a referee's whistle for a foul call. The Oregon style of aggressive, slashing play led to frayed nerves and occasional outbursts by players and coaches, but UCLA performed as a veteran team should, playing its own game and letting Oregon pick up most of the fouls. The Bruins had things well in control midway into the second half and won decisively, 84–66. Walton stood out in usual fashion with 25 points, 19 rebounds, and 9 assists, while Dave Meyers had one of his best efforts, scoring 22 points and giving Bill strong support on the boards. The next night Oregon lost again to USC and fell two games off the pace.

The very next week the Bruins looked like a vastly different team. They traveled to Oregon and lost two straight games to the state's Pac-8 entries. Both games were close and low-scoring as first Oregon State and then Oregon used stall tactics to combat the high-powered Bruin offense. Mainly, though, it seemed as if UCLA had lost its poise, panicking as the other teams wiped out UCLA leads to tie or go in front and passed poorly or missed easy lay-ups. The Oregon State defeat, 61–57, was particularly surprising since OSU was a "green" squad with mostly freshman as starters that had already lost 10 games. That result gave heart to Oregon, which came back from its trouncing of the previous week to throttle UCLA's offense and eke out a 51–46 win.

With that "lost weekend" UCLA was out of first poll position and certain not to regain it for the rest of the regular season. The team even was in danger of losing the conference race and the chance to defend its national title in the NCAA tournament. The national guessing game among basketball experts began on the question of "What's wrong with the Walton Gang?" There were suggestions that perhaps Wooden hadn't kept up with the times by staying with his predictable styles of offense and defense. One or two observers thought Walton was not playing with his usual flair, but the statistics indicated he surely was pulling his weight. More often it was the guard play that came in for hard knocks.

American Basketball Association scout Lionel Purcell told reporters, "In football, you don't win titles without strong offensive tackles and guards are like tackles. The UCLA point guard is terminating his penetration too high, and this creates extended passing lanes instead of compressing the defense in a normal operating manner. It takes you out of a regular motion."

Another ABA scout, Bill Bertka, agreed. "With what is, ostensibly, a one-guard offense, there is a lot of pressure on Curtis bringing the ball up the court. The defense isn't trying to steal it, but wants him to give the ball up to Meyers or Wilkes, who, as forwards, aren't playmakers."

A few commentators restressed what might have seemed obvious. The law of averages tends to catch up with any player or team. Other teams had excellent players who could, on occasion, use their talents at close to 100 percent efficiency. Coach Bill Mulligan of Riverside College said, "So UCLA loses to the pretty good teams in a vicious area and everyone is worrying about them. That's a tribute to their great record."

Walton and Company said little but went back to intensive scrimmages to prepare for the stretch drive. And then, just as many experts were writing them off, they found themselves again. In rapid succession, with Walton twisting, hooking, running as well as ever and the guards showing the fire and spirit that had seemed lost, UCLA overpowered both the Washington teams, California, and Stanford and, finally, walloped USC. With those wins, the Bruins ranked as number two nationally behind North Carolina State going into the NCAA regionals.

Bill had closed out his Pac-8 college career on a high note. The UCLA drubbing of USC still ranks as one of the best exhibitions of team basketball by any squad against a worthy opponent. The question of fans' lips as the regionals started was which UCLA group would show up: the superteam that had thrashed USC, North Carolina State, and Notre Dame or the mistake-prone quintet that had lost seemingly safe leads in the closing minutes against Notre Dame, Oregon, and Oregon State.

The first pairing seemed to indicate the Walton Gang was back as Walton played an excellent game and the other Bruins performed well in easing past their first opponent. Now only the University of Dayton stood in the way of a Bruin trip to Greensboro, North Carolina, where they figured to be the favorite to win an eighth-straight title.

Dayton was a good team with a fine, but "small" six-eight center and able shooters and ball handlers. But it wasn't a great team. On past performance it didn't seem to have the board strength to stay with the Bruins. Some sportswriters thought Dayton might try a stall, the most logical method for a team having to cope with Walton and the other high-scoring UCLAns. But Dayton used a run-and-shoot offense and had rarely tried a slowdown game. The Flyers' coach decided to let his team play its normal game.

For a while it seemed the wrong thing to do as UCLA threatened to break the game open on several occasions. But the Flyers stayed close and began to draw closer and closer to the Bruins as the second half reached its late stages, an ominously familiar pattern in this season. In the last few minutes the pace grew hectic as the teams traded baskets time after time and the crowd, mostly rooting for the underdog, reached a frantic pitch. In the last minute Dayton scored to break a 78-all tie; then UCLA pulled itself together to tie the game with fourteen seconds to go. Both benches were up and yelling and the arena was in an uproar as Dayton got ready to bring the ball in for the last shot that could shatter UCLA's last streak, the 37 straight in NCAA competition.

The Dayton coach signaled time-out to work out last-second strategy, but for precious seconds some of the Flyers didn't see him. Just as some of the Dayton players caught the officials eye with the T signals, the man with the ball, scoring ace Pete Smith, headed for the basket and let fly with a set shot. The crowd saw the ball swish through the net for what seemed like the winning basket and erupted in yells, cheers, and wild activity. But the officials had called time just before the shot, and the basket was ruled out. Dayton brought it in again and got off one shot, but the fates seemed in UCLA's corner, and the game went into overtime.

The Bruins weren't safe at home yet. The teams continued to match scores as the five minutes went by. With half a minute to play, the score stood at 96–all. Then Sylvester of Dayton hit to make it 98–96 UCLA responded quickly as they brought the ball down fast and Walton set a pick that let Greg Lee hit to tie it up with twenty-two seconds left. Now Dayton decided to go for the last shot again. The guards and forwards passed the ball around as the clock ticked down to fourteen seconds, thirteen, twelve, ten. Then the pass came to Smith in the corner, and he tried to pass to center Fisher in the low post with nine seconds left. Fisher seemed free, but just as the ball headed toward him, a long arm flashed out to knock the ball away.

Walton followed the block by rushing past a straining Dayton man to retrieve the ball. Then he startled the crowd by dribbling toward the midcourt line with the agility of a guard. The clock kept running down— six seconds, five. There was no time for Bill to do anything but shoot. On the run Walton cast off a long arching shot that hit the peak of its trajectory and slanted down toward the basket as the buzzer sounded for the first overtime. For Dayton fans the passage of the ball seemed an eternity. It came down, hit the glass backboard, and just missed going in. Dayton was still alive, but no one could deny the big redhead had made a magnificent attempt.

Though Walton had played the entire game, he seemed to be gaining strength as the second overtime started. He shook hands with Fisher, then rose high above him on the tap, twisting around in midair to catch the ball with his fingertips and slap it back to Greg Lee. Lee deftly brought the ball into Dayton territory, setting up a score that put UCLA in front to stay. With Walton becoming increasingly dominating on both boards, UCLA moved away from a weary Dayton team that had played its heart out and had come within an eyelash of keeping UCLA out of the finals for the first time in nine years.

Now UCLA headed east for the last showdown game of Walton's college career. The luck of the draw placed what promised to be the college game of the year in the semifinals. North Carolina State awaited the Bruins, yearning for revenge. They were number one and UCLA number two in the ratings, but the single loss on their record had been the humiliating one inflicted by the Walton Gang in St. Louis.

For the state of North Carolina it was like a crusade. Thousands came out every day in State's hometown of Raleigh, 80 miles from Greensboro, to watch the Wolfpack practice, cheering loudly when Burleson, Monty Towe, or David Thompson made a particularly sparkling move in a scrimmage. Newspapers urged the team on in editorial columns, and some churches even offered up prayers for their success.

Outwardly at least, UCLA was calm. Following coach Wooden's usual approach, the team held all its practices behind closed doors and the players made few comments to the press. Walton drew curious stares off court as he went around in T-shirt and jeans, wearing sandals and often carrying a bag of fruit, but he said nothing to reporters. A few statements reached the press from the Bruins. Coach Wooden used some psychology as he suggested: "I want State to remember that eighteen-point margin." Andre McCarter told a reporter he didn't think at all about losing: "I won't believe it. It just doesn't fit into history."

When the two teams went through their final warm-ups the day of the game, every seat was filled, mostly with Wolfpack supporters who roared out State cheers and occasionally sent piercing rebel yells on high. But there had been empty space a little earlier when Marquette outlasted the University of Kansas for the right to play in the championship game two days later. Most observers felt whoever won the State-Bruins struggle would take the title—and subsequent events proved them right.

Finally, the preliminaries were finished. The pregame interviews had helped whet the interest of a national TV audience of 50,000,000 to 60,000,000, and the teams had been introduced. The audience rose to its feet in unison as Walton and Tom Burleson squared off in the center circle. The ball went up, and the first omen seemed in UCLA's favor as Walton got the tip and swatted the ball into the backcourt. A hustling Dave Meyers picked it up, helped bring it into the attacking zone. The pass went to Walton, who scored the opening points of the contest. North Carolina State quickly evened things as Burleson went over Walton with a well-executed hook shot.

Seconds later Walton retaliated with a hook, but North Carolina State scored on its possession. The teams seemed evenly balanced, and the early tempo set the tone of the game. The lead seesawed back and forth constantly. UCLA went ahead, 12–10, but the Wolfpack ran off five to lead, 15–12. State held the lead at 21–18 a little later, when a field goal by McCarter followed by two foul shots by Wilkes put UCLA in front 22–21. Then Thompson responded with a dazzling display of talent, leaping high in the air as though to try a field goal, then catching the Bruins off guard with a midair pass to Burleson, who put in an easy two-pointer to bring State in front, 23–22.

And so it went throughout the first half as the crowd nervously moved around, up and down in its seats in rhythm with the furious pace of the game. Near the end of the half the Wolfpack broke out to a 29–24 lead. Then Walton soared high above several State basket guardians to tip in a missed Bruin shot and was fouled by Thompson in the process, setting up a three-point play. Little Monty Towe brought the ball back and sank a long-range shot for 31–27, but Greg Lee responded with a field goal to close the gap again. Then Burleson took a pass in deep on Walton, and the seven-four giant pivoted perfectly around Walton to make it 33–31. Moe Rivers hit for State—35–31, but Wilkes scored to make it 35–33. State tried to work for the last shot as the clock ticked away toward the end of the half but lost the ball.

With six seconds left, Lee brought the ball in, then passed to Dave Meyers. Meyers was far away from the basket as the second hands showed five seconds left, four, three. Then he put all his strength into a desperate heave that sped toward the State basket from 45 feet out. Before the ball reached the backboard, the buzzer sounded, but the sphere banked in perfectly for a dead-even contest at the half.

At the start of the second half, with Walton leading the way with board control, shot blocks, sharp passing, and good scoring moves, UCLA looked like the fearsome team of legend. The Walton Gang ripped through State defenses to a 57–46 lead. Some of the massed ranks of sportswriters from all sections of the United States started thinking about what superlatives were left to describe another Walton Gang triumph. But just as suddenly, the Wolfpack bounced back, with Towe's midgetlike frame weaving in and out of the sweating Bruins defenders as he drove the baseline or whipped off eye-of-the-needle-threading passes to teammates all over the court. The Wolfpack ran off 10 unanswered points before Dave Meyers hit a jumper to end his team's dry spell at 59–56. As the packed arena crowd screamed approval, State responded to make it 59–58. After Wilkes sank a field goal, Towe drove the baseline for two points, then the Wolfpack got the ball back and set up a three-point play as Thompson made an incredible leaping shot and drew a foul at the same time: 62–61. At the other end Walton fed Meyers beautifully, and the rangy forward put UCLA on top again by a point. The Wolfpack soon tied the game on a foul shot with four minutes to play.

After the Bruins failed to score, Carolina changed its strategy, going into a stall. As the tension mounted, the minutes seemed to drag by as the Wolfpack slowly worked the ball around the outer perimeter of the attacking zone without taking a shot. Greg Lee finally fouled Thompson trying for a steal, but the dynamic State star made one of his rare misses. UCLA went to Walton, who put in the lead basket as the clock showed less than a minute to play. The Wolfpack refused to fold. A lob pass to Thompon was converted into a tying basket, 65-all. UCLA still had sufficient time to take the game, but the Bruins couldn't hold onto the ball. With seconds to go, Carolina had the opportunity to go for the last shot. Wolfpack fans pleaded for the team to sew it up; some crossed their fingers or prayed silently. With under ten seconds to go, State's Stoddard got loose in the corner, set, and pumped. The ball wasn't quite true. It hit the rim, and UCLA got the rebound. UCLA missed a last frantic shot, and regulation time expired.

The tension was terrific for every one. This time State got the ball and worked it in to Burleson. Walton blocked his way, but he made good use of his height advantage to get the ball in over the Red Baron. UCLA came right back to tie it at 67 as Lee hit from the corner. Then, when the Wolfpack failed to score and UCLA got the ball, it seemed likely the tide might swing their way. Lee and Curtis brought the ball up as the crowd shrieked for Wolfpack defense. Suddenly Stoddard lunged forward to intercept Lee's pass, and now State once more went into its stall.

The ferment increased as the seconds went by and UCLA, fearful of fouling, had to guard closely but carefully. Everyone knew it would probably boil down to one more shot, and Walton tried to brace his team with shouts of encouragement as he fought for position with Burleson. The scoreboard showed a half minute, twenty seconds, ten seconds, and suddenly the State offense galvanized for the hoped-for kill. The ball went to Thompson, brilliant all night, who drove for the basket, stopped, and whipped it to Burleson.

Big Tom clenched his teeth and rose high above the basket for a short spinning toss. The ball hit the rim and caromed off into UCLA hands as the buzzer resounded again. In five minutes of extra time, two of the highest-scoring teams in the nation had managed to put in two points apiece.

The cheers, fight songs, and band music continued to swirl around the arena as the second overtime started. The UCLA dynasty had tottered as it had the week before, but somehow the gods had smiled, and the Walton Gang still could pull through. It seemed as though this might be so as Walton helped spark the Bruins to a string of points right after the jump. UCLA got the ball, and when a field goal try missed, Bill, Burleson, and Meyers converged on the basket.

Walton couldn't quite tip it in, but Burleson was caught reaching in over Bill's shoulder. Walton calmly went to the line and sank both free throws. After State failed to score, the Bruins went to Bill out from the basket. Ten feet from the hoop, Walton executed a stylish fallaway jumper to make the score 71–67. The pressure seemed to be getting to Carolina as it once more failed on offense and a defender fouled Wilkes in the act of shooting for another three-point play.

Gloom started to settle in on the partisan audience. It looked as though the fearsome Walton Gang steamroller had been unleashed. But then, as had happened in South Bend two months before, UCLA went into reverse. Tommy Curtis, overeagerly trying to get the ball from little Towe, fouled him, and Towe responded with two foul shots. Then Towe returned the favor by fouling Tommy, but the usually reliable Curtis could make only one point. As the crowd roared with renewed hope, the Wolfpack went on the attack. A groan arose when a shot hit the basket and bounced back, but David Thompson found superspring in his legs to propel his six-four frame above the tall Bruin basket guardians to tip it in. But with only two minutes to go, a four-point margin still was plenty if the Bruins maintained their heralded poise.

This time the law of averages caught up with them. Suddenly it was UCLA, not its foes, that succumbed to last-minute shakes. A turnover let Carolina work around the basket, where Burleson pushed in a tip in to make it 75–73. Then Walton threw the ball away and moments later fouled Burleson, who sank one shot.

Seconds later State fouled Meyers in the forecourt to set up a one-and-one. If Dave converted, it seemed likely the Bruins would survive. But he missed the front end, and State got the rebound. The arena was bedlam as Thompson got in close and sank an eight-foot bank shot that gave his team a lead it never relinquished.

As the emotionally drained crowd fidgeted through the final minute, the Wolfpack managed to stave off frantic Bruin scrambling, to end the Bruins' seven-year reign 80–77.

The mighty had fallen, but there was nothing to be ashamed of. The game had been one of the most memorable ever played in college ball, a classic in every way that could have been won by either team many times in the long evening. Burleson had been far more effective against Walton than earlier in the season. Still, the stats showed Bill had done his part—he had scored 18 points to 14 for Tom and outrebounded him, 29–20. Perhaps the more significant factor was the Wilkes-Thompson matchup. In the earlier game Keith had outperformed the All-America junior by a wide margin on both offense and defense. In Greensboro, Keith had one of his rare off nights, making only 5 baskets in 17 tries while Thompson rolled up a game-high 28.

Walton took it as he normally did. He congratulated the Wolfpack players and consoled his own team. After getting dressed, he went out and signed some autographs for children before moving toward the exit to his stoop-shouldered way. As reporters followed hoping for a last-minute word, he stopped to shake hands with a man in overalls who said, "I work here and I just want to shake your hand."

Walton responded, "Thanks and thanks for all you've done for us."

The *Sports Illustrated* reporter wrote: "As the redhead walked out of college basketball and into the evening drizzle the game could say the same to him. At the end Bill Walton didn't even need to win. He had already fit [sic] into history."

9 Battle of Legends

In Philadelphia, Pennsylvania, and Portland, Oregon, in the spring of 1974, excited fans looked forward to a coin toss. It was, in fact, one of the most expensive coin flips in history, for the winner was certain to pay well over $1,000,000 for the services of William Theodore Walton.

But to the owners of the professional basketball franchises in those cities at opposite ends of America, it seemed cheap at the price. The Philadelphia 76ers and Portland Trail Blazers had earned the right to contend for Bill's services by having two of the worst records in the National Basketball Association in 1973–74. But history had shown what having a great center could do. Milwaukee had signed Kareem Abdul-Jabbar and become one of the perennial contenders for the NBA title. Walton seemed capable of doing the same for his new club.

Officials of the two clubs and the NBA met, shook hands, and tossed the coin. It spun up in the air, the lights of the conference room glinting off it, then came down as every head craned to see whether heads or tails showed up. The NBA president gave the word—Portland had won and beaming Trail Blazer officials whooped for joy, shaking hands all around as photographers snapped pictures for front-page stories in hometown papers.

More headlines came soon after as Sam Gilbert, representing the Red Baron, and Portland team owners worked out contract terms. When those sessions ended Walton was an instant multimillionaire. The agreement called for Bill to play for the Blazers for five years for a total stipend of $2,000,000. At a news conference Bill softly told reporters he was well satisfied with the arrangements and looked forward to testing his skills against the best talent basketball had to offer.

On several occasions Bill stressed he wanted to play pro ball for the challenge of it; the money was secondary. However, he indicated he felt he deserved to be paid what he was worth just on principle. He expressed his basic feelings on salaries for pro athletes to *Newsday* correspondent Jay Weiner in early 1975:

"I think athletes are underpaid. The largest group of professional athletes are big-time college football and basketball players and, at best, they only get a few thousand dollars a year [through scholarships]. Through circumstances, like in professional basketball, a few of us make very large incomes. Still, we wouldn't be paid these salaries unless the owners felt it was in their best interest. Our salaries reflect the extraordinary emphasis on spectator sports and the huge sums of money our labor generates. Unfortunately, the people who participate in sports, who generate all this income, are not receiving the profits."

To Weiner's query about who was making most of the money, Walton replied, "Owners of teams are making money. TV is making money. And *Sports Illustrated* is certainly making money."

These remarks might have shaken some observers who had not followed Walton's occasional comments about his social views during his college years. In early 1974, for instance, he told a Los Angeles *Times* reporter, "My political beliefs are socialist. I think everyone should have an equal share and shouldn't be given special favors and have more things just because they do something that . . . happens to be good."

Some critics in turn suggested that Walton offer proof of his feelings by donating to charity much of the huge salary he had negotiated with Portland.

In Portland, orders for season tickets came in steadily, while reporters spent the months between the end of the 1973–74 season and the start of the next one by wondering what would happen when Walton confronted the other famous graduate of the Wooden basketball school, Milwaukee Buck star Kareem Abdul-Jabbar.

Asked to compare his two famous protégés, John Wooden began by calling them the "two most maneuverable men of that size I've ever seen. In personality, Kareem is a little more withdrawn, not as much outgoing as Bill. But both are great team players. That's what makes a big man stand out if he has ability.

"Lewis is a little stronger physically and at least

three inches taller, that's considerable, and he probably has a little more reach. Bill has a little better timing [particularly] at initiating the outlet pass as far as the fast break is concerned. Size makes [Jabbar] a little better, but Bill has the advantage of being a little more maneuverable. In rebounding, Bill is a little more maneuverable in going after the ball. He also practices with a little more reckless abandon."

As the summer went by, optimism reigned in Portland. Citizens of the "rose capital of the world" looked forward eagerly to a season in which one of their teams would bask in the national sports limelight. Cash registers clicked steadily in Trail Blazer offices as season ticket sales went past 3,000, 4,000, 5,000 and, before play started, past 6,000. Before Walton even stepped on the court in a Trail Blazers uniform, the management was assured of at least two-thirds capacity for every home game.

Some experts reserved judgment. They warned that the transition from college to pro ball is never easy for a player, no matter what his background. For a free spirit like Walton who put so much emphasis on the enjoyment of athletics, it might prove doubly difficult. Pro ball, they pointed out, was not just a sport; it was a business. Athletes in such leagues as the NBA knew that if they faltered, they didn't just stand to lose a place on a team, but a job, often the only job they knew. It is a case of survival of the fittest in every sense, they noted, and there wasn't anything playful about the physical punishment players meted out to each other in the struggle for dominance. In addition,

Walton's condition remained a question mark. He underwent surgery after the college season to correct some of his knee problems, and he still had some twinges in his back.

On the surface, at least, none of this seemed to bother him. He had a relaxed summer in his usual fashion, bicycling and backpacking. He seemed to enjoy the streams and woodland of the Oregon countryside and spent some of his time looking for a place to live that would be secluded, yet not too far from the city. Eventually he settled for a large A-frame house set in the middle of a large wooded tract.

In response to his team's desire for good publicity, he talked to reporters more often, though he still reserved most of his leisure time for his own pursuits. He emphasized that basketball remained his main pleasure. Bicycling was worthwhile, he noted. "You go out there, have a good workout with friends, break a sweat. I like bicycling. It helps the mind. But basketball is the most fun. I am looking forward to it. I look forward to everything I do.

"I've spent the summer mostly moving around. I don't make plans. I do what I have to do on a given day and see what comes out." But the date he always kept in mind, he indicated, was September 12, the start of Portland's rookie camp.

When he showed up to start his pro career, he met a new coach. During the summer Portland had changed coaches, bringing in the veteran player, a certain Hall of Famer of the future, Lenny Wilkens. The courtwise Wilkens already had some coaching experience in

Seattle, where he ran the Supersonics pro team for several years as player-coach. Wilkens still was an excellent playmaker and figured to help sharpen Walton's understanding of pro styles of play through actual game situations.

Wilkens and Portland management knew that the team really was considerably better than its 1973–74 record might indicate. An expansion team, it had been operating for only a few years, and many of its players were only approaching the experience normally needed to cope with such longtime kingpins as the Boston Celtics, New York Knicks, or Los Angeles Lakers. The nucleus of a fine squad was already there even without Walton. For one, the Blazers had another former UCLA great at forward, Sidney Wicks. His game had improved every year, and already he was rated one of the best in the NBA. At guard, besides Wilkens' occasional chores, there was a standout ball handler and field goal artist named Geoff Petrie, who was usually good for 20 to 30 points a game. The rest of the team also had ability in line with most of the squads in the league. A good year for Walton, then, promised to provide Portland with its first entry into the NBA championship play-offs in team history.

Walton trained as hard as anyone on the roster as the initial practice sessions moved along. Coach Wilkens told reporters he was pleased with his big man's progress and hopeful for the season ahead. For Walton, it was a strange situation. Despite his years of stardom in college ball, he was once more an unknown quantity. He was a rookie again, and he had to prove himself all over. Unlike most newcomers to pro basketball, he was fighting time. The great majority of freshman pros had the advantage of anonymity. No matter how sensational their college accomplishments, they were obscured by the established stars of their new team. They normally had at least a few years to find themselves, to become accustomed to the strains of topflight competition before moving onto center stage.

But Walton was in a fishbowl. The eyes of fans in every city were on him, expecting him to learn overnight what others required years to do. After all, they said, look at Jabbar. He made the Milwaukee franchise in a single season. And Jabbar was the measuring stick; millions of people awaited the confrontation between these living legends to evaluate Big Bill's worth.

Their first meeting was to be in an exhibition game in early October. In between, though, Walton was scheduled to play with the Blazers in several other exhibitions. The first of these was in Los Angeles in late September against the Lakers. At the pregame press conference, newspaper reporters, magazine correspondents, and TV teams thronged a hotel conference room, a huge gathering drawn by one of the rare chances to direct face-to-face questions at the usually elusive Walton.

There was a babble of voices and the whir of TV cameras as he walked slowly in, looking sheepishly away from the crowd and carrying his lunch—mainly a container of orange juice—in a brown paper bag.

No longer required to meet the Wooden dress code, Bill wore his hair long, his flowing locks held in place with a blue print scarf. He looked more like a repairman than an athlete, dressed as he was in a green plaid shirt, gray slacks, and brown work shoes.

Most of the questions were predictable. One reporter asked about his weight, referring to the effects of Bill's vegetarian diet on his physical condition. "I can't say how much I weigh. But I weigh more at a comparative stage of the season than I ever have."

What about his hair length and scraggly red beard? "I kind of anticipated that when I left UCLA that sort of thing wouldn't be important anymore. I've done a lot of thinking about the importance that's placed on the length of one's hair. It's not my trip."

Would his life-style blend with the hectic pace of the NBA? "It's not my job to worry about that. You might spend a lot of time worrying about it. I don't."

The subject of basketball almost seemed an after-thought. But Bill did get to comment on his coach ("Lenny Wilkens is a beautiful man") and his first pro game ever: "It will be nice to get out there and play against a lot of new faces."

Bill got a warm welcome from the crowd, many of whom had watched the redhead during his glory years at UCLA. In the game Walton didn't do badly against the Lakers' seven-foot center, Elmore Smith. On the other hand, he didn't control the tempo either. However, he got his share of rebounds, scored points, and made some fine passes to his teammates. For his first try at big-league ball it was a creditable performance.

However, both teams were in early stages of training and were trying out new players and patterns. Los Angeles, besides, was missing some of its personnel because of injuries and wasn't the well-oiled machine of the Jerry West-Wilt Chamberlain years. A better test was promised when the Blazers went east to play the Bucks.

The game was scheduled on what amounted to a neutral court, the University of Dayton arena in Ohio. Long before the teams arrived, newspaper stories had inspired local fans' interest as had posters advertising the "First Historic Meeting—Jabbar vs. Walton." Even as Walton got his baptism of fire in Los Angeles, tickets for the Milwaukee exhibition were available only at scalper's prices. When the two squads began their pregame drills that October evening, a capacity crowd of 13,458 was looking for a game more like the NCAA finals than a meaningless practice contest. The idea of these two supercenters facing each other fired the national imagination as well. Television crews sweated to get the cables and cameras in position to send the game back to viewers in Los Angeles, Milwaukee, and Portland, and people in other cities were disappointed they couldn't sit in as well.

When the referee walked to midcourt and the two towering forms moved toward the tip-off circle, the audience let out a sustained roar that seemed loud enough to shatter the TV lenses. Walton held his hand out to his taller adversary, grinned, and said "Hi, big fella." Kareem responded cordially and proceeded to win the jump. Soon after he took a pass in his favorite

143

spot five feet from the basket, turned, and deftly put the ball in over Walton's straining arms. Walton got Kareem on the arm as the taller man went up and was called for a foul.

It was the start of a long evening for Big Bill as Kareem put on a scoring show, hitting the cords almost every time he took a shot, dunking the ball from close in on several occasions and dropping in a sweeping hook from as far as 10 to 15 feet out every now and then. Twenty seconds into the second quarter Jabbar drew gasps from the crowd as he demonstrated his renowned sky hook from 17 feet out, the ball settling into the net without touching the rim. On defense, too, Jabbar played impeccably, flyswatting the ball away to thwart Blazer outside shots and battling his younger opponent for every loose ball.

And yet, though Kareem obviously took the night's honors, it wasn't that one-sided. Walton was outscored, 34 to 15, but Bill played the high post, and many of his shots were taken from the key or beyond. And he did tally 15, second only to Sidney Wickes in Blazer scoring. On the boards, although Jabbar made more spectacular plays, Walton actually outrebounded Karem, 16–11. The game wasn't a runaway. At the half Milwaukee held only a 49–48 lead and the final margin for the Bucks was 103–96.

John Wooden told a reporter he wasn't surprised at the outcome. Walton had 5 pro games against Kareem's 500, an experience edge in Jabbar's favor that "is almost immeasurable." The game, said Lenny Wilkens, was a learning experience for Bill. "Believe

144

me, in this league no guy can stop another guy one-on-one. And when that guy is Jabbar and his opponent has never played a league game, it's unfair."

It was true that Bill hadn't been able to stop Jabbar's famous sky hook, a high arching shot Kareem could direct to the basket with radarlike accuracy from almost any point in the attacking zone. But then, neither could such acknowledged stellar centers as Boston's Dave Cowens or Chicago's Nate Thurmond.

Kareem told a reporter that Walton was a talent and would be first-rate when he learned the pro grame. But he did think too much was made of the matchup. "Comparisons . . . are very special to the press, but it's beyond me to create a mythical rivalry."

Bill's opportunity to add to his education proved to be limited, though. Only a few weeks into the season he began to be troubled by a bone spur on his ankle. He left the team for medical treatments, and rumors started to fly that there was great dissension on the team, that Walton wanted to be traded, that Bill was malingering when he could be playing. Bill remained silent through much of this, traveling to Los Angeles for treatments, then retiring to his Portland home to read and talk to close friends. Undoubtedly some of his teammates felt resentful; they had counted on Bill to make the team into a title contender, and the season was slipping away with little to show for it.

But some voices were raised in Bill's behalf. Willie Naulls, a respected businessman and once a star center on UCLA himself, wrote the Los Angeles *Times:*

It seems the sports press has gone very sour on Bill Walton. From what I gather, this seems to be fed by almost anything, from a silly and overblown disagreement with a friend and the fact he has retained a lawyer to such trivia as his eating habits, the color of his hair and the fact that he has house guests. Sports must have its color, and apparently Bill has been selected for the darker tones.

But let's not cloud the history of the man, or the statistics of the games. In all this speculation about malingering, isn't there one writer who remembers that Walton wanted to play badly enough that he sat in ice packs before games and after and during halftime so he could run on his wretched knees? Or that he played with a severely injured back when the NCAA championship was at stake in 1974? . . .

Finally, Bill broke his silence. He might have made some statements to friends he thought were in confidence when he was feeling depressed about his problems. But he wanted to play and wanted to help his team. He tried to demonstrate this in the most effective way, by returning for a time in early 1975 to rejoin the Blazers before his ankle started acting up once more and sidelined him again.

One of the first stages of his return was his first league start against Kareem. The results weren't very different from the preseason event. Jabbar won the battle of the statistics by a sizable margin. But the game was close most of the way, and Walton gave flashes of his old brilliance every now and then. A lot of articles and sports commentaries dealt with the way Kareem took Bill's measure in that one game, but few gave much attention to what happened afterward . . . or before.

Though Kareem was still a problem, Walton demonstrated he might have something to say about NBA matters in later seasons. He played an excellent game against such distinguished players as Nate Thurmond of the Chicago Bulls and Bob Lanier of the Detroit Pistons. Against Chicago, in a losing effort, Bill scored 20 points and grabbed 13 rebounds. Detroit also won, but it was a nip-and-tuck struggle that wasn't decided until a Piston star hit a field goal at the final buzzer.

Perhaps more significant was Bill's first home game after his ankle injury. The crowd of 10,580 gave him a rousing standing ovation when he came on the court for a game against Philadelphia's 76ers. The 76ers, though they'd lost the toss for Bill, were greatly improved and no longer the doormat they'd been the year before. But buoyed by the cheers of the fans, Walton put on one of his best professional performances: controlling the backboards as of old and scoring consistently from the field and under the basket. While the scoreboard glittered with the final 119–97 Blazer victory margin, thousands remained in the arena to watch Bill discuss his feelings in a postgame interview on the Trail Blazer radio network.

Bill took the opportunity to address the crowd. He waved at them and flashed a warm smile. "I appreciate the reception," he said. "It was real nice to get the good support of the people. Some places thought I really was a bad guy. It is nice to play and I hope we can put a bunch of wings together and accomplish our goal of winning the Pacific Division."

There were only 3,000 to 4,000 fans left, but they yelled until they were hoarse and clapped their hands until the flesh was red. Bill left the floor with volleys of cheers ringing in his ears. Later, after showering and dressing, he stood for many minutes talking to Portland youngsters and signing autographs.

10   Center of Controversy

The careers of most college superstars follow one of two patterns once they move on to pro ranks. They may continue to dominate their sport and make the headlines for outstanding performances and/or salary disputes. Or they prove vulnerable to the pressures and slowly fade from public attention.

Walton's odyssey took a vastly different turn as he made the front pages around the country for reasons having nothing to do with basketball. Apparently, however, he was an innocent bystander rather than a chief participant in events that made news.

Hardly had the frustrating 1974-75 Trail Blazer season ended when two of Walton's close friends, who shared his home in Oregon, were investigated by the F.B.I. for possible involvement in the Patty Hearst case. There was speculation that the two—controversial one-time Oberlin College athletic director Jack Scott and his wife Micki—might have helped the girl and her kidnappers-turned-associates, Bill and Emily Harris, hide from F.B.I. pursuit. Walton was questioned, as were many friends and acquaintances of his and the Scotts. The Scotts admitted no wrongdoing. There never was any intimation that Walton himself had anything to do with the Hearst case. Rather, his name became involved because of his friendship with the Scotts.

In early April, 1975, the Scotts and Walton held a news conference in San Francisco in which they claimed the government law enforcement agency was harassing them unduly. In his remarks Bill called the F.B.I. the "enemy" and said, "I would like to urge the people of the world to stand with us in our rejection of the United States Government."

The response from most quarters was quick and angry. Sportswriters, columnists and TV sportscasters almost universally noted that Walton was attacking a system that made it possible for him to earn millions of dollars. The Trail Blazers censured their prodigal son, "deploring" his statements and declaring that "The United States is the freest and most democratic nation in the world. We and people throughout the world recognize this. . . . We believe the National Basketball Association is an example of the opportunity available to people under our form of government and Walton, more than most, has reaped extraordinary benefits from this system."

A few days later Walton said it wasn't true that he opposed the system. "It's important that what we mean by [our statements] is that it's not the American people or the Constitution or anything, it's the recent government trends in this country, primarily the Nixon-

Mitchell-Haldeman-Erlichman gang and now the gang of Ford-Kissinger-Rockefeller. Given their actions and their politics, I have a moral obligation not to do anything to cooperate with them."

At the same time he stressed his continued love for basketball. He had decided to move to Oregon, he told reporters, "leave all my friends. . . . and decided that I liked basketball enough that I would sacrifice those things.

"I'm playing basketball and it just so happens that they pay me two million dollars for it. That doesn't mean that I'm required to sacrifice my morals or anything else.

"Regardless of what other people think, I have to do what I think is best. It just so happens that some people don't like what I say, but that doesn't mean I'm wrong. This has nothing to do with basketball. I've felt this way for a good part of my life."

Some newsmen sought out Coach Wooden for his comments. Wooden said, "Bill is not a leader. I feel he has been misguided and misled, but I still feel he is as interested in his fellow humans as you or I."

Later, while attending a basketball clinic in Massachusetts, Wooden told another interviewer, "Some of the things Walton has done have been horrible. I'm critical of them and so should you be. . . . Give me two hours alone with Bill and I will get him on the right track. The trouble is, give some other guy two hours after me and Bill's gone again. . . .But I won't cast him out. Others have; oh yes, they have. But I won't. He's mine, one of my boys, and always will be no matter what happens."

As the year went by, minor items about Bill appeared here and there. There were rumors, about whether he would play for Portland the next season, be traded, or retire. Some sportswriters suggested he would have to play for Portland if he played at all because he had become too "controversial" for most other teams. As a diversion, Bill served as a guest disc jockey for a Portland radio station for five hours and got a big kick out of it.

Then, on August 6, he joined in a news conference in New York with the Scotts who were faced with a possible summons to a Pennsylvania grand jury proceeding in the Hearst matter. The main thrust of the conference was similar to the previous one. They planned "total noncollaboration with the U.S. government and its police agencies."

Walton, his long red locks billowing down his shoulders, wearing a khaki shirt, faded green shorts and sandals, enlivened the proceedings with a critique of the ranks of reporters and TV cameramen gathered around him: "It's obvious that you folks have been lied to for a major portion of your lives. Look at your dress, the way you live, the way you deal with other people. So much of it is a lie—one contradiction after another. . . . I think it's about time that some of you folks start drawing some better conclusions about what's coming down in this country. 'Cause I think a lot of people in the press must, you know, be listening to those lies that they've been told too many times in their lives."

For a rock fan, the words had a familiar ring to them. They carried the message of Bob Dylan's "Times They are A-Changin' " and Walton is known to be a rock devotee who admires Dylan and Country Joe McDonald among others. But the Dylan song was written at the start of the 1960s, and times already had changed. Certainly no basketball player fifteen years earlier would have imagined getting millions in pay for a few seasons of work or taking part in such an unusual press meeting.

The question remained at the end of the otherwise uneventful summer whether Walton would be remembered as a basketball player turned political activist or a free spirit who also could play Hall-of-Fame basketball.

Only a few days after the New York conference there were indications that Bill might still have some athletic dreams. Reports from Oregon, where he maintained his residence despite many reports that he hated the drizzly nature of the northwest, were that Bill had increased his vegetarian intake to raise his playing weight. A friend of his told a reporter that Bill had increased his weight to 240 pounds and was aiming for 260 while keeping to his meat-free regimen of vegetables, fruits and nuts, seeds, grains, herbs and juices. "The others had finished [the meal]," the informant said, "but Bill continued to eat his vegetable specialties for a full two hours. He does it every day, slowly but surely adding sustenance beyond his normal intake."

Walton said he was following some advice given him by Wilt Chamberlain and he planned to have the muscle needed to cope with the bruising centers of the NBA.

"I'm going to be much more aggressive this season," he was quoted as saying. "I want to show what Bill Walton can really do!"

INDEX

157

West, Jerry, 80–81
Westfall, Wes, 94
Westra, Mike, 8, 10, 11, 89
Whitehead, Sam, 71, 72
Wicks, Sidney, 42, 43, 50, 57, 99, 103, 140
Wilkens, Lenny, 139–40, 142, 144–45
Wilkes, Keith, 8, 10, 11, 13, 47, 50, 51, 52, 58, 63, 65, 66, 67, 73, 75, 78, 82, 86, 87, 88, 90, 92, 109, 111, 112, 118, 119, 122, 128, 129, 132, 133
Williams, Gus, 8
Witte, Luke, 69, 70
Wooden, John, 8, 14, 15, 18, 33, 34–44, 46, 52–55, 56, 59–60, 62–64, 66, 72 ff., 82 ff., 102, 109, 113, 114, 115, 116, 117, 119–20, 127, 137–38, 144, 151–52
Woolpert, Phil, 103, 104

The Author

Irwin Stambler is an avid sports fan as well as a widely known author in the automotive and aviation field. He, his wife, and children live in Beverly Hills, California. Among his popular books from Putnam's are *The Supercars and the Men Who Race Them,* *Great Moments in Stock Car Racing,* and *Automobiles of the Future.*